FOLLOW ›TO LEAD›

STAN O. GLEASON

FOLLOW **LEAD** »
» TO

— THE JOURNEY OF A DISCIPLE MAKER —

WORD AFLAME PRESS
WELDON SPRING, MO

Word Aflame Press
36 Research Park Court
Weldon Spring, MO 63304
pentecostalpublishing.com

Cover design by Elizabeth Loyd

26 25 24 23 22 21 20 19 18 17   1 2 3 4 5

Library of Congress Cataloging-in-Publication Data

Names: Gleason, Stan O., 1957- author.
Title: Follow to lead : the journey of a disciple maker/ by
    Stan O. Gleason.
Description: Weldon Spring : Word Aflame Press, 2016.
Identifiers: LCCN 2016046188 (print) | LCCN 2016046786
    (ebook) | ISBN 9780757752209 (alk. paper) |
    ISBN 9780757752346 (spanish : alk. paper) | ISBN
    9780757752216 () | ISBN 9780757752353 (Spanish)
Subjects: LCSH: Discipling (Christianity)
Classification: LCC BV4520 .G57 2016 (print) | LCC BV4520
    (ebook) | DDC 253--dc23
LC record available at https://lccn.loc.gov/2016046188

This book is dedicated to my parents, Wendell and Rea Gleason, whose lives of integrity and modeling made Apostolic disciples out of their four children, Gary, Pat, Pam, and Stan.

TABLE OF CONTENTS

FOREWORD

When we are born in the natural, it is impossible for that life to survive on its own. Of necessity, parental protection, teaching, admonishment, exampling, and love are the contributing factors ensuring survival of human life. Within the animal kingdom, these exact same ingredients are exhibited and executed to ensure the survival of the species.

The unspoken feeling among many is that when you receive the baptism of the Holy Ghost, you have arrived. No, you have just entered into a whole new way of life. Without teaching and discipleship from the Shepherd and those qualified in ministry, the new convert has no hope of survival in the kingdom of God!

The necessities listed above are of utmost importance for the survival of the spiritual man as well as the man in human growth and life.

As we hold these instructions in our hands, and read from these pages, suddenly it becomes like a light that shines down on an otherwise clouded pathway.

The soul is the seat of the human will, intellect, and emotions. Only God Himself will be able to register the innumerable lives that will have been discipled because of this disciple who speaks experientially on the Master's command to "go and make disciples of all nations" (Matthew 28:19, NIV).

I bow my knee to this great accomplishment. There are many instructors as the apostle Paul admonished, but not many fathers. Herein we feel the "spirit of father."

I have known this author and his lovely family for over fifty years. Thank you, Stan Gleason, for this masterpiece—author and friend!

– Lee Stoneking

PREFACE

The greatest living thing in the world today is the church of Jesus Christ. There is no other organization or entity on earth that can even come close to having the impact the church has delivered in terms of the implications for all humanity—past, present, and for eternity. Jesus Christ, the founder of the church, left His followers with a purpose, a plan, and a product. Now, millenniums after the birth of the church, we must ask ourselves the hard questions: Are we accomplishing the vision of the Founder? Are we employing the method He modeled to accomplish His desired purpose? Is the product that we're yielding identical to the original? When we are willing to ask these questions and are courageous enough to revisit the original blueprint of the mission He gave, only then can we discover whether the church is on task or if the plan has been altered.

It is painful and troubling to realize that the present rate of church growth is not keeping pace with the increase in the world's population. The job ahead of us is overwhelming, but not insurmountable. I am not so naive as to believe that I have a corner on the market for worldwide revival or that I hold the long undiscovered secret on how to reach the world. I have no expectations that this work alone will change how the church does the business of reaching the world, but perhaps it can help us better understand how the first-century church was so successful.

Jesus spoke words just prior to His ascension that made Heaven shout and Hell shudder: "Go therefore and make disciples of all the nations" (Matthew 28:19). Every Christian that has read this text can clearly identify it as the Great Commission. Fulfilling the Great Commission is the essential practice for the church that demonstrates how we value what was accomplished for us on the cross. His great sacrifice is our salvation (Romans 5:8), His great grace is our motivation (Philippians 2:13), and His great lifestyle is our method to fulfill His vision (Matthew 11:19).

Did Jesus actually think that His small band of followers could achieve what He tasked them to do—to reach every nation, even the most remote regions of the world? And what redemptive potential did Jesus envision for His followers to possess? Could they realistically make disciples out of every person in the world, or at least a high percentage of the population? Did He overestimate His power within them or the job He had done to equip them for their mission? Did He misjudge their ability to accomplish this task? Was He leading them along with false bravado and a naive imagination?

Jesus was a master teacher and well understood the principle of taking His students from what they knew to what they did not know. Early on as they followed their Rabbi, the disciples did not picture themselves as great and powerful leaders of an exponentially expanding church, but they did know fishing. Perhaps the only tangible demonstration Jesus gave His disciples concerning what real revival looked like, sounded like, and felt like was the miraculous catch of fish in Luke 5.

With all of their human ingenuity, skills, and experience, their all-night fishing expedition had yielded nothing. At a command from the Master, "Launch out into the deep and let down your nets" (Luke 5:4), their lives changed forever. Suddenly, all kinds of fish rushed into their net causing it to break. As they hauled in this miraculous catch, their boat began to sink. The harvest was so massive that it required sharing their bounty with another boat, and that one began to sink too. As the disciples gawked at their unprecedented and unexpected breakthrough, it was undeniably clear to them that they could not take credit for this supernatural harvest.

Capturing this teachable moment, Jesus identified the ultimate purpose for the miraculous demonstration: "From now on you will catch men" (Luke 5:10). This miracle was not about giving His disciples bragging rights down at the pier, providing a bonus for their labor, or enabling their early retirement. The only lesson attached to this miracle of purpose was to acquaint His followers with the magnitude of their future. They were going to make an impact on the world with this kind of far-reaching force. When the Day of Pentecost revival hit Jerusalem, they would better understand what Jesus was teaching them by this miracle.

What was their take-away from this miracle in relation to the Great Commission? If they connected their abundant catch to the future, they certainly had a sense that they were headed toward something really big. They also may have begun to understand that what they would do for Jesus involved human ability, but clearly they would be supernaturally directed and empowered by God. Their future catch of people would be unprecedented and worthy of celebration. Before this prophetic miracle could be fulfilled in their future ministry, they would be required to obey the directives of the voice of the Lord. They would have to be willing to launch out into the deep if necessary. Jesus did not tell Peter how deep deep was. That was left to his discernment, but apparently he calculated the correct depth, and so must we.

The disciples would have to be willing to receive whatever kind of fish God sent into their net. Their net might break and some fish might be spilled, possibly meaning that not all their catch would be fully discipled. Their boat might sink, requiring partnership with another boat, meaning their future revival would be shared and networked. And ultimately, their catch would be so big they could not take any of the glory for it. Peter fell at Jesus' feet and said, "Depart from me, for I am a sinful man, O Lord" (Luke 5:8). When true revival comes, it will be so great and so overwhelming that anyone would be a fool to attempt to usurp God's glory. Few today have ever seen a revival like this, but I believe that an end-time revival of biblical proportions is here, and we must be ready to disciple it.

In the fall of 2012 I was praying and asking the Lord to speak to my heart about the vision He wanted for our local church in the coming year. I felt as though He clearly spoke into my spirit the words, "Go make disciples." I was temporarily stunned and felt a little taken aback (I'm ashamed to admit). My flesh wanted to respond with, "Okay, duh . . . I've been trying to make disciples my entire adult life. What else do You have for me?" I thought I knew all there was to know about making disciples. I had been reasonably successful at seeing unbelievers become committed saints of God during my years of ministry. I had never called it "making disciples" nor did I think of the Bible studies

I taught as making disciples, but at that moment I felt a great expectation about what God was trying to say to me. I quickly dispelled my sarcasm and continued to pray over those words. The Lord seemed to let me know that I had much to learn about how He wanted me to fulfill His Great Commission.

A few days later I attended a small Christian leadership conference in Kansas City. The facilitator of the conference asked those in attendance to state their names and share their spheres of ministry. One man stood and said that his vision was to come alongside churches and help them make disciples. I thought, "*Hmmm, this may be a cue card.*" I took him aside during the break and, after a brief but intriguing discussion, invited him to lunch. To shorten the story, over the next eighteen months he partnered with us to help train and develop a disciple-making culture in our local church. Now three years later we still have a long way to go, but by the grace of God we have made great progress in embedding a disciple-making culture in our local church. I am humbled and honored to share part of our journey in this book. I have included his name and contact information in the notes at the end of this book. I'm also happy to report that I was privileged to baptize him and his wife and now they call me "pastor." For this I give God all the glory!

This book is not an attempt to tout the final and ultimate missing tool for church growth. The intent is simply to bring the reader back to the original intent of Jesus' command to go make disciples and to grasp a fuller range of the meaning of that command. I am suggesting that we have not yet fully discovered how to implement this critical command. Many of our well-meaning methods of evangelism have undoubtedly served the mission, but we have unwittingly masked the Master's intended method and fallen short of the goal.

It is critical to any Christian practice that we first have proper theological understanding. The Lord said that His people were suffering from insufficient information (Hosea 4:6). Thought always precipitates action. Defective orthodoxy will always produce flawed orthopraxy. If we can get our theology and terminology right, then maybe we can change the missional practice of the church and actually accomplish the mission of Christ before His soon return. Is there something missing in the daily practice of the twenty-first-century saints of God? I believe generally that there is.

In this work we will investigate the rabbi-disciple culture of the first century. This will give us a background of understanding regarding the meaning of the mission to make disciples. We will discover what it meant to be a disciple of Jesus Christ in the first century and see how the twenty-first century is doing by comparison. We will revisit the forty-two months of Jesus' earthly ministry and discover how He was able to build the foundation of a church in such a short period of time that has now lasted nearly two thousand years. We will attempt to deconstruct every possible excuse that well-meaning but uninformed Christians have presented to exempt them from answering Christ's command to make disciples. We will discover the cost of making disciples and realize that there is a great price to pay in answering Jesus' call to "follow Me" (Luke 18:22).

We will take a close look at our own lives in an attempt to determine if we think a prospective disciple would find us worth following. We will also discover the Monday through Saturday disciple-making mentality that elevates Sunday to a whole new level. We will examine the question that was asked of Jesus, "Who is my neighbor?" and discover that the answer to this question has significant implications for local, national, and worldwide social harmony. We will address great discrepancies between the soulwinning model and the disciple-making model and discover the vast difference in long-term impact. Finally, we will explore some practical applications of disciple making in an effort to provoke thought and discussion within your local church.

What's my { Purpose Place Where do I Belong

CHAPTER 1

GO MAKE DISCIPLES:
THEOLOGY PRODUCES BIOGRAPHY

Thinking precipitates behavior. Proverbs 23:7 says, "For as he thinks in his heart, so is he." It has been said that "when we sow a thought we reap a behavior. When we sow a behavior we reap a character. And when we sow a character we reap a destiny." A blessed destiny begins with a biblically correct thought.

If reaching the world is the destiny of the church, then we must think the right thoughts about how to fulfill that purpose. What is our theological approach to reaching the world? Should we all just do whatever comes to mind to reach others with the gospel, or perhaps copy what other churches or organizations are doing that seems to be working to reach the world? If a vehicle is not operated according to the specification of the owner's manual, then the performance of that vehicle will be something less than what the designer intended. Notwithstanding Paul's admonition to by all means save some (I Corinthians 9:22), surely the Founder of the church not only gave us power to reach the world but also equipped us with His strategy to do so.

Much has been done to reach lost people through the invention and inspiration of humans and with some measure of success. Everyone is interested in something that is working. I have had countless conversations with pastors about what they are doing to make an impact in their communities. It is human nature to emulate successful mentors or models that have resulted in great growth. Sometimes God inspires certain individuals in unique ways to reach the lost, but He may not intend for that method to become a theological track to perpetually follow. Moses first met God at a burning bush, but he did not keep looking for God behind every bush he saw.

Brilliant people with great hearts for God have devised means to reach lost people and marketed their ideas with great success. Countless congregations have jumped on the bandwagon of a local church's success, purchased its materials, hit the streets, and enjoyed some results, but eventually the enthusiasm waned and it was back to business as usual. I have had people recommend books to me that I was eager to sit down and read. On more than one occasion my high expectations were not met and I was severely disappointed in the material. My frustration taught me that a book is only as good as where you are in life when you read it. If a book that someone recommended to me is not talking to me, I have learned to place it on the shelf and wait for that season of my life to unfold before I pick it back up. Someone else's inspiration can easily become your frustration as you attempt to duplicate his or her success. God may have spoken to that person about a particular plan, program, or initiative, but He did not speak to you. No one is guaranteed success simply by following someone else's model.

God inspires pastors on how to make an impact in their communities. He places a congregation in a community with unique gifts, qualities, vision, skills, talent, resources, and leadership specifically equipped to become fruitful in that area. Each message to the seven churches of Asia in Revelation 2 and 3 was individually suited to that particular congregation. One method of outreach may work in a certain community but has absolutely no impact in another. Rather than borrow from successful church models or read books about how to be effective in reaching particular demographics and cultures, doesn't it stand to reason that God would have given us a method that would work in any century, on any continent, in any local church, and in any culture? Well, the good news is He has!

Before we can have the right practice in our local congregation concerning fulfilling the Great Commission, we must first have the right theology. Having the wrong theology is sort of like not getting the first button of a shirt pushed through the corresponding buttonhole. If the first button is not inserted into the right place, then the entire garment will appear disheveled and will not look like what the designer envisioned. Jesus said in Matthew 6:33, "But seek first the kingdom of God and His righteousness, and all these things shall be added to you." If theology is right, then everything else in Scripture fits and life will fall into place. If our theology is wrong, then a multiplicity of problems will follow. A correct theology in our minds should produce the appropriate biography in our lives.

If we, as the church, are to engage the most effective practice in making an impact on the world around us, then we must first have the right understanding of Scripture. In His command, "Go make disciples of all nations," Jesus gave us the right theology. If His idea of reaching the world with the gospel is correctly interpreted theologically and then biographically enacted, we will be successful in doing what God has called us to do. If we do not understand, or have somehow missed the full meaning of His instructions concerning how we are to reach the world, then we will not be equipped with the full power available to us. Consequently, the results will not be as fruitful as Christ intended.

It is my belief that Christ's commission to go make disciples has not been completely understood by Christianity as a whole and among some Oneness Pentecostals in particular. That is not to say that many of our efforts in reaching lost people have not been useful or effective. But as we stand on the cusp of the soon return of Christ and are overwhelmed with the urgency of all the work yet to be done, it would be expedient to reexamine all that is enfolded into the command, "Go make disciples."

Perhaps we still have much to learn concerning the method that Jesus modeled and made sustainable within His disciple-making culture. We have so many more advantages to reach this world with the gospel that were not afforded to our apostolic ancestors. Their travel was difficult and their communication was slow. But contained in the command, "Go make disciples," was a timeless method that, when employed, provided a strategy to reach the world within one generation of time.

Do we have the right theology? We claim that we do, and it is certainly so regarding the essential doctrines of the Godhead, new birth, and Apostolic identity. Oneness Pentecostals (also referred to as "Apostolics" in this book) typically contend that they lay no claim to embracing any religious tradition, but the truth is, we can be as traditional as any other denomination. For example, don't we usually sit in our "assigned" seats every Sunday? Paul wrote, "Therefore, brethren, stand fast and hold the traditions which you were taught, whether by word or our epistle" (II Thessalonians 2:15). Not all tradition is bad.

Tradition that is rooted in Scripture will always be right although it may need to be refreshed and personally owned by each succeeding generation. Heritage is what our ancestors leave us, but an inheritance is the living faith of our forebears abiding within us. Tradition may become counterproductive when ineffective programs and methods are protected by local church stockholders who believe that some things are too sacred to change. Never mind that the church atmosphere is stagnant and these ineffective programs and methods aren't helping anyone, changing lives, or influencing the community.

One tradition Pentecostals adopted years ago was the use of hymnals. I remember when some in the church were worried that we would become charismatic if we threw our hymnals away, not considering the fact that we got them from the Methodists. One out-of-town visitor who came to our church from another Apostolic church was convinced we were backslid because we did not use hymnals, but projected the words to the worship choruses on a screen. Where did we get the idea for kneeling and tarrying at the altar (mourners' benches)? Did the apostles use these, or did they receive the Holy Spirit "where they were sitting" (Acts 2:2)? Is it apostolic that 100 percent of religious activity happens behind the closed doors of the worship facility, and only the professional staff does the work of the ministry?

We have historically prided ourselves in bringing nothing into our Pentecostal worship experience from the older denominations. However this simply is not true: we borrowed hymnals and mourners' benches from the Methodists, Sunday school from the Baptists, and worship facility architectural design from the historic church (i.e., long narrow sanctuaries with rows of pews and high, ornate lecterns). Most of our worship songs come from Charismatic and Evangelical artists, not to mention that some hymn tunes were adapted from worldly songs. We may not be as free from tradition as we would suppose.

Fellowship was a critical component to the success of the early church, but there does not seem to be much fellowship that occurs on any given Sunday in a Pentecostal church. And yet the Book of the Acts of the Apostles, our model and standard, clearly says that the first-century believers faithfully ascribed to the apostles' doctrine and fellowship (Acts 2:42, 46). True biblical fellowship is more than meeting at Pizza Hut after church and just having a good time. Fellowship in Scripture is the Greek word *koinonia,* which infers a mutual and common exchange of hearts, faith, and experience. This simply does not happen on Sundays in America. Most worship experiences (including some Pentecostal churches) are one-dimensional with the professional clergy going through the motions behind elaborate pulpits while the audience mindlessly stares at the hairdos in front of them as they nod their heads in approval.

In the first-century church, the expectation and the experience was that all born-again believers did ministry. Originally, the word *minister* was a verb and not a noun. Somewhere Christianity turned an action word into a title. The fivefold ministry (see Ephesians 4:11) provided leadership for the church, but ministry was shared by all. Saints were trusted to serve, and they were highly esteemed by their leaders. The apostles equipped, empowered (i.e., laid on hands and shared their authority), and released saints for ministry. One example is the development of deacons in Acts 6. Notice what happened when the seven were identified, ordained, and commissioned: "And the word of God increased; and the number of the disciples multiplied in Jerusalem greatly; and a great company of the priests were obedient to the faith" (Acts 6:7). When the ministry was decentralized and the saints were equipped, empowered, and released to do ministry, the results were explosive.

It is a wonderful thing when the saints believe in the pastor, but it is even more wonderful when the pastor believes in the saints. The historic church does not have a legacy of leadership that believed in and empowered church members for ministry. For most of church history, there was a gap between ministerial professionals (educated clergy) and parishioners (mostly theologically uneducated laity). Peter and John would have never been respected spiritual leaders, much less apostles, in the historic church. Their trained antagonists referred to them as unlearned and ignorant men (Acts 4:13).

The clergy were the interpreters of Scripture. They told the laity what the Scripture said, what it meant, and what they should think about it. Some churches today may not specifically use these terms but they function somewhat similarly. The church members do not think for themselves, neither are they allowed to make simple decisions without consulting their pastor. The pastor may tell members if and when they can take vacations, how they should spend their money (beyond biblical stewardship), and what color of carpet to install in their homes. This style of pastoring does not trust the laity to do any ministry except to clean the church or cut the grass. This kind of leadership will stunt spiritual and numerical growth.

Jesus did not intend for His command to "go make disciples of all nations" to be fulfilled only by the fivefold ministry or the so-called professional clergy. This was a commission for every believer to embrace. In fact, Acts 8 presents a paradigm shift in fulfilling Christ's vision. Following the death of Stephen, intense persecution came against the church. The last phrase of verse 1 says, "And they were all scattered throughout the regions of Judea and Samaria, except the apostles." It appears that this persecution served as the catalyst to launch the gospel beyond the city limits of Jerusalem.

The narrative states that the apostles remained in Jerusalem while other believers suddenly became refugees and were randomly dispersed throughout many communities of the region. One might say this effort was launched through the tyranny of the urgent (like the WWII fighter pilot who said he made his first parachute jump when his plane was shot down). Saul continued to persecute the Christians, which further dispersed them to far-reaching areas. Then verse 4 makes a startling statement that perhaps would upset the theological applecart of some today: "Therefore those who were scattered went everywhere preaching the word." So if the apostles remained in Jerusalem, and it was the church members who were scattered during this persecution, then it appears that the ones who went everywhere preaching the Word were the saints. Apparently these non-licensed but obedient saints were qualified and empowered by the apostles to take what they had been taught and repeat it to everyone who would listen.

The privilege and responsibility of preaching (communicating) the Word does not belong to the fivefold ministry alone. Saints may not be called preachers, but they may take in what they hear on Sunday and from pastoral Bible studies and carry it outside of the four walls of the worship center, rehearsing it to anyone who will listen. I would venture an educated guess that the overwhelming majority of ministry that takes place in most of our churches occurs within the walls of the worship center or on campus. Yet the model we have been presented with is for the saints to go everywhere throughout the week preaching the Word.

Too much ministry is being done by the church for the church. We continually carry the water to the river instead of to the desert. In the beginning it was not so. Most of the ministry in the first century was done beyond the walls. In fact, the first dedicated Christian edifice was not built until the third century. However, the lack of a regular worship space did not seem to hinder the spread of Christianity. What would happen in the Apostolic church today if everyone did the work of the ministry and the majority of ministry occurred beyond the walls of the worship center? It is no mystery why a local congregation will grow proportionally to the percentage of ministry that is done by the saints beyond the walls of the sanctuary.

Those early believers did not have buildings to focus their lifestyle around. They did not see themselves as people who went to church; they believed they were the church everywhere they went. For them, church was not a destination but a journey. For them, church was not a facility but an action. They did more church in streets and in homes than they did in sanctuaries.

Where did they get this model? Clearly their example was Jesus. They had watched Him work far more miracles and do more ministry in the streets, in the fields, at the lake, and in homes than He did in the synagogue or Temple.

We must not put all of our ministry eggs in one basket called Sunday. According to Acts 2:47, "the Lord added to the church daily those who were being saved." There is only one possible explanation for why they were able to enjoy daily conversions. A few verses earlier it says, "So continuing daily with one accord in the temple, and breaking bread from house to house." The Lord could add daily to the church because the first-century church was a daily church. Not very many of our local churches have reached the activity level of being a daily church, but when we do, the Lord will begin adding daily to the church.

I constantly remind our local church that what happens Monday through Saturday is more important than what happens on Sunday. If we are not doing what we have been called and commissioned to do the other days of the week, then Sunday has a different purpose. When Sunday is the only ministry day of the week it becomes a pep rally or motivational meeting where everyone gets propped up so they can go back out into the world and do nothing purposeful to build the kingdom of God. In a way, it's like ordering at the counter of a fast food restaurant. Before you place your order they want to know, "Is this for here or to go?" When we come to church most people order for "here" and don't get it "to go." But Jesus' vision was, "Get it to go!"

If we are doing the work of the ministry and are making disciples Monday through Saturday, then Sunday will not be a therapy session for codependent saints. Sunday will become a celebration of thanksgiving for all the great things that God is doing through His people to fulfill His mission. Nothing will excite a congregation like sharing real-life stories about making disciples and seeing lives dramatically changed. If we get our theology right and do what we should be doing Monday through Saturday, then Sunday will be an important part of an entire life of worship.

Questions for discussion:

- What are some nonessential traditions we observe? How can they be a hindrance and not a help?

- Can you think of an example of a ministry that happens outside the walls of the local church building?

- What are some things that stop us from taking ministry outside of the church walls?

CHAPTER 2

FIRST-CENTURY DISCIPLE-MAKING CULTURE:

DON'T REINVENT THE WHEEL

What if you were presented with a challenge to launch a company with a vision to make an impact on the entire world and given unlimited resources to get it done, but only given three years to initiate and establish your new enterprise? How would you accomplish this seemingly impossible task? With unlimited technology and communication venues available today, the choices to get your message out are endless. Of course, the biggest challenges would be to make sure you establish the vision and values of your company beyond your short season of influence and that your company is built to last. Obviously, you would have no guarantees that your work would outlive you, but neither did Jesus.

Would you immediately rent billboards, buy television advertising time, or induce mass social media blitzes? Would you attempt to attract the largest audiences possible and use any means necessary to convince consumers that your company could be trusted and your product valued? Would you write a book or produce a series of videos and distribute your training to anyone who would listen? All of these strategies and more have been employed to launch new companies with great success. But none of these plans could accomplish what Jesus came to do; He had a much different business plan.

As the Lamb slain from the foundation of the world, Jesus had a date with destiny. He came to die alone, but not as a one-man show. He gave His life as a sacrifice for us when He was in His prime. Launching His ministry at age thirty, He had forty-two months to get done what He came to do. He could not afford to waste time, make mistakes, or experiment with unproven methods. He would leave a legacy, but more than that, it would be necessary for Him to establish His vision, values, and virtues on this earth in a tangible manner. He could not do this by speaking to large crowds or by writing books. He understood that He could not make a lasting impact from a distance. He would need to do something more enduring than delivering sermons from the mount and working notable miracles. The real work He came to do had to be on a small scale that involved personally investing in individuals.

What Jesus came to establish would need to outlive Him and not be a "one and done" proposition. He had to install a method to perpetuate His mission beyond one generation. He needed to leave behind a way of life that would last for ages to come. He didn't have a lifetime to do it. It is truly remarkable that He fulfilled His mission and built a sustainable model within three-and-a-half years. His prophetic clock was ticking, for He would have to die on Passover, resurrect on First Fruits, and pour out the Holy Spirit on Pentecost. His calendar was set; therefore, every day needed to count and urgency pulsated in His every action.

The last words from someone on his or her death-bed are treasured and preserved forever by their doting loved ones. The final words that Jesus spoke while physically here on earth were uttered immediately prior to His ascension. What would He say at this critical and impressionable moment? We call His final speech "The Great Commission." Jesus could have chosen this critical setting to utter many things, knowing that His words would be forever embedded upon the collective psyche of His most ardent followers. Contained within the Great Commission are Jesus' last words, "Go make disciples."

Matthew 28:19 renders the mission and the model of the Founder's plan for His followers to reach the world with His message. The King James and the New King James versions identify four commands contained in the Great Commission: go, baptize, teach, and make. The church has done a relatively good job of obeying the first three but we have fallen short in the last. Only one of these commands actually develops a disciple: make! This three-word command from the Lord to "go make disciples" was an invitation for the disciples to begin living their lives with purpose and intention. Although perhaps they did not fully grasp the long-term implications of His initial invitation to "follow" Him, there was an implied expectation that they would do something significant with the investment He would make in them.

When Jesus said, "Go make disciples," His vision was not lost on the hearers. First-century dwellers in the land of Israel were well acquainted with the rabbi-disciple relationship. After carefully choosing their followers, rabbis would spend their lives teaching, training, imparting, and sharing their lives, values, and principles. This is how the Lord Himself lived, and His disciples followed His model during their ministries. The Second Temple era was characterized by a disciple-making culture. Disciples would follow their rabbis endlessly down dirt roads and across hillsides. It was said that they were collecting the dust from their masters' feet. Disciples did not choose their rabbis but the rabbis chose their disciples by frequenting the synagogues and rabbinical schools, searching for Israel's brightest and best young men.

The Scripture does not say it, but it is unlikely that Jesus would have gone to the synagogues to search for His followers. Perhaps due to His lack of reputation, experience, and young age, Jesus instead went to the seashore, the pier, tax-collecting money tables, and searched under fig trees for His followers. Numerous times in the gospel accounts Jesus said, "Follow me." He was not reluctant or ashamed to invite followers into close proximity. They had no earthly idea what awaited them behind the door He was opening unto them, but Jesus knew. He was inviting them into a close, endearing fraternity where their lives would be changed forever, and in turn they would change the world.

When a rabbi uttered the words, "Follow me," both he and his invitee understood that the rabbi was offering his life—his wisdom, learning, knowledge, and experience. The disciple's part of the agreement included a commitment to follow, the hope of a more informed and educated life, and when the time was right, to someday begin perpetuating his knowledge by inviting others to follow him.

The first-century church was more relational and less institutional in nature than the twenty-first-century church. The early church continued daily in the Temple and from house to house; they shared their resources and did ministry together. The emphasis on relational disciple making is what empowered the church to grow rapidly and spread like wildfire around the known world. This model, however, became lost throughout the centuries of church history, and eventually the church failed to be a people-building culture. Instead, congregations came to be built around personalities and buildings with a transition toward a programmatic approach to fulfilling the mission of Christ. Large, ornate structures created congregations that gathered primarily to observe the leaders go through their liturgical motions. These one-dimensional meetings built powerful leaders but failed to equip and nurture common Christians. As an unfortunate consequence, the concept of New Testament fellowship was largely lost. Nonbiblical language emerged, and terms like clergy and laity created an institutional dynamic that separated church leaders from church members.

Consequently, disciple making and relationship building gradually diminished and were replaced with an easier and less cumbersome paradigm of edifice- and personality-driven worship events. Could the lost model of building relationships explain why church polity evolved into a hierarchy, thus establishing a great gulf between the professional clergy and the so-called unlearned and ignorant laity? The tragic trickle-down effect was the lost art and lifestyle of disciple making.

Jesus uttered numerous powerful statements to the disciples immediately prior to His departure. In Acts 1:1–8, Jesus told them to go back into Jerusalem and wait for the promise of the Father, that they would receive power after the Holy Spirit had come upon them, and that they would be witnesses unto Him locally (Jerusalem), regionally (Judea), cross-culturally (Samaria), and internationally (uttermost part of the earth). This vision of their future was captivating and compelling, but it was contingent on His command for them to go and make disciples. The command to go and make disciples must become the overarching theme of the church with which all other principles, practices, and purposes align. No leader, personality, program, or institutional initiative can or should ever attempt to replace the plain language and vision of the purchaser and founder of the church. Jesus never told us to go build programs, buildings, or massive congregations, but simply to go make disciples.

If someone asked you if you were a Christian, you probably wouldn't give it a second thought before you answered, "Yes." However, if someone asked you if you were a disciple, would you be as quick to answer? Isn't this a much different question? We are well-acquainted with the term *Christian* but not nearly so acquainted with the word *disciple*. I would venture to say that the term disciple conjures up images of the twelve bearded and long-robed followers of Jesus. In our usage today, the closest we typically come to the word disciple is in discipleship. However, even this usage often refers to a group of new believers that meets weekly to listen to a teacher tell them what the major doctrines of the Bible are, and how they should be living their lives. Although such a class is important, this system falls short of the biblical model of making disciples. No one is capable of making twenty or thirty disciples all at one time. Disciples must be made like Stradivarius made violins, one at a time.

How would a twenty-first century disciple compare to a first-century disciple? Generally speaking, the expectations placed upon Christians today by leadership in the church are considerably different than the expectations that Christ and rabbis of His day placed upon their disciples. Today, our basic expectation is for sinners to become born-again, come out of sin and the world, faithfully attend church, and hopefully become faithful stewards of their calendar and finances. Most pastors would be delighted if they could achieve this level of commitment from their church members.

If a pastor today asked the congregation, "Are you a Christian?" the majority would quickly and without much thought raise their hands. But if a pastor asked, "Are you a disciple?" the response might be confusion or a blank stare. That pastor may receive the same response Jesus received: many walked away. Being a Christian speaks generally about what Christ did on the cross for us, but being a disciple is more about how we respond to the cross with every area of our lives. Perhaps the real question should be, "Does my lifestyle as a Christian qualify me to be a disciple?" I believe that I could make a strong argument, and will attempt to do so later in this book, that the definition of a disciple includes making disciples. That is, if we are not making disciples, then we are not disciples ourselves.

We have lost the identity and the profile of a disciple today. Identifying as a Christian has come to mean something different than what following Christ meant in the first century. Jesus said in Luke 14:26–27, "If anyone comes to Me and does not hate his father and mother, wife and children, brothers and sisters, yes, and his own life also, he cannot be My disciple. And whoever does not bear his cross and come after Me cannot be My disciple." Then He added a postscript in verse 33, "So likewise, whoever of you does not forsake all that he has cannot be My disciple." Based on these words we can confidently say that Jesus placed expectations, if not demands, on His disciples. We could take it one step further and observe that Jesus disqualified potential disciples (or more accurately they disqualified themselves) that did not meet His expectations of discipleship.

Jesus did not have a multilevel organization with classes of disciples who had achieved various graduated qualifications. He had disciples who followed Him closely and met His definition of a disciple. He also had multitudes that followed Him from afar but were not held to the same standard. The average local church is much the same; levels of commitment vary widely. What would happen to a local fellowship if a culture of disciple making was woven into every fiber of activity? What if every ministry director personally made disciples and had a priority of making disciples? What if the pastor and his or her spouse personally made disciples and modeled that practice weekly before their congregants?

The message Jesus gave to us in Matthew 5–7 and 25 is compelling and should be taken to heart. In response to His message in these chapters there has been a strong move in Christianity in recent years to embrace a kind of "social gospel" by providing food, clothing, and shelter to individuals in need. Historically, the Apostolic church has not always been strong in the area of serving and blessing the community. As honorable and impressive as these humanitarian efforts are, they were not the primary mission of Christ followers in the first century and they should not be our primary focus today.

I remember my dad telling a story about a fire department that was contacted to rescue a cat from the highest branches of a tree. The neighborhood gathered with intrigue to watch the heroic exploits of the firemen. The ladder was completely extended while one man reached as far as he could for the cat. To the roar and applause of an approving audience he gently procured the little kitty from its precarious perch, returned to the ground, and proudly placed the feline in the grateful and relieved arms of a tearful little girl. The firemen smiled and swelled with pride as they accepted congratulations for their heroic act and climbed into the firetruck as the spectators waved and applauded again. No one noticed, however, that the little girl had let the cat down on the ground and as the fire truck was leaving, it backed up over the cat. There is tragedy, humor, and irony in this story and it makes me think of the many heroic humanitarian efforts that the church has substituted for true disciple-ship. We all feel good about ourselves for digging wells, serving in soup kitchens, and initiating clothing drives, but when it's over, have we made any disciples?

The main point of being a disciple of Jesus Christ is not to become a member of a church, ascribe to a code or creed, or check the boxes of all the possible philanthropic pursuits. The priority of Jesus and His disciples was the lost world He came to save. God did not become human flesh to feed and clothe the world. His priority was to seek and to save the lost. In fact, Jesus demonstrated His priority by addressing spiritual issues before physical needs when He first forgave sins and then healed. (See Matthew 9:2.) That being said, it should be noted that, with few exceptions, the main focus of Jesus' ministry was not to save sinners. He forgave the sins of the paralytic, He refused to condemn the woman taken in the act of adultery, and He assured the thief on the cross that he would soon join Him in Paradise. Paul said that Christ committed the ministry of reconciliation unto *us*. Christ's work as the Redeemer did not officially begin until after His ascension, and that work is exclusively accomplished through His disciples going and making disciples, as they are enabled by the Holy Spirit.

Please do not misunderstand me. I believe humanitarian efforts are important. But these efforts do not, by themselves, fulfill the Great Commission. They may ease people's pain for a day or two, but if we do not include disciple making in the process, then we have done little more than provide temporary relief. The old saying applies: "Give a man a fish and he will hunger again, but teach a man to fish and he will never be hungry." Every humanitarian effort should have a disciple-making strategy built into it. This should not be interpreted as being manipulative or disingenuous. In my opinion, Jesus had an agenda when He fed the five thousand. He invited them all to follow Him by making an appeal for their commitment. As was the case in John 6, the appeal to commit doesn't always work out, but at least the invitation should be given.

We do not have the advantage of the first-century disciple-making culture when we talk about reaching the world. There is a reason Jesus declared and then instituted the propagation of the gospel through the disciple-making model. That reason is the power of building relationships with the people we want to see saved. We cannot ship salvation to people like corporate America ships products to customers whom they will never meet. The gospel must be personally delivered to the door of every heart by a disciple maker who has caught the vision of Jesus Christ to do His work, His way.

Questions for discussion:

- What qualities do you think Jesus was looking for when He chose His disciples?

- What is the difference between using programs to meet needs and building relationships to make disciples?

- What do you think is the difference between being a Christian and being a disciple?

CHAPTER 3

LIVING
INTENTIONALLY:
A LIFE WORTH REPRODUCING

You can live for God and have good morals, joy, and fulfillment in Christ. But if you are not taking someone on the journey with you, then you have not discovered your ultimate purpose as a disciple. Someone making disciples is also doing all of that but he or she has learned the dimension of living an intentional life. I heard about someone who hung a sign on his bedroom wall that said, "When my feet hit the floor the devil says, 'Oh no, he's up again.'" We achieve Hell's attention when we involve ourselves in the lives of sinners, friends, unbelievers, and new believers. Disciple makers who are living their lives deliberately for others pose the greatest threat to Hell's agenda.

Making disciples means having a front row seat as you watch the grace of God develop lasting spiritual fruit within believers (John 15:16). Disciple making is the most exciting life in the world. It has been said that if you love your job then you never have to work a day in your life. Using the same expression, if you love to make disciples, then you never have to go to church a day in your life because you bring church with you everywhere you go. Keep in mind that the first-century church did not worship predominantly in one dedicated space. Acts 5:42 says, "And daily in the temple, and in every house, they did not cease teaching and preaching Jesus as the Christ." Teaching and preaching Jesus Christ sounds like doing and being the church because whenever you talk about Jesus, He shows up.

The first-century disciples did not live their lives intentionally one day a week while on their way to corporate worship. They did not go to one particular central address once a week to *do* ministry. They ministered daily and from house to house (Acts 2:46; 5:42; 16:34, 40; 20:20; 21:8). "Every house" (Acts 5:42) appears to indicate either believers opened their homes to provide a disciple-making opportunity or perhaps a systematic movement through neighborhoods (whether believers' homes or not) making sure they did not miss any future potential disciples or families. It is no small wonder that according to the Acts narrative, the Jerusalem church numbered in the thousands (Acts 2:41; 4:4; 5:14; 6:7). They sowed bountifully and therefore reaped bountifully.

Obviously, nothing can take the place of corporate worship. In fact, serious disciples understand that they must be an integral part of a local congregation that provides vision, accountability, spiritual covering, and structure. In the twenty-first century we have the best of both worlds of public worship (temple) and private worship (house). The best place for vision, correction, direction, and inspiration is the public house of worship. But the best place to make disciples on a relational and fellowship level is in a private setting like a house. In such a location there is comfort, intimacy, a controlled environment, and yes, some food. The early disciples frequently broke bread together. Food can be spiritual if it is intentionally structured around Christ-centered relationships.

Believers not engaged in disciple making may be living for God, but they are not living intentionally so as to fulfill the mission of Jesus Christ. I would venture a guess that the vast majority of Apostolic believers do not consciously have continual thoughts about potential disciples God may place in their paths on a daily basis. Too many believers miss the cue cards posted by God's stagehands for potential disciple-making opportunities. I once heard a believer with a heart for lost people say, "I go to the grocery store to meet people for Christ, and while I'm there I may pick up some groceries." Once we make the commitment to spend our lives making disciples, we can never just randomly go or be anywhere. Having a disciple maker's heart means seeing a person and saying, "There you are." The greatest tragedy of a sanctified life is to never live intentionally for others with a heart to make disciples out of them.

There are several Scripture verses that speak to intentional living: Psalm 37:23 says, "The steps of a good man are ordered by the LORD, and He delights in his way." Proverbs 3:5–6 says, "Trust in the LORD with all your heart, and lean not on your own understanding; in all your ways acknowledge Him, and He shall direct your paths." Based on these two passages alone, it is apparent that God orders and directs the daily path of each of His children. Here's what we know: God loves lost people and He wants to reach them with His saving grace. And He deliberately planned for us to help Him do that. So if He has His mind on someone who needs to be saved, He may choose you or me to get His message to them. This can happen in one of two ways: God can direct us to a specific place, house, street corner, vending machine, office, parking lot, and so on, or He can put us on assignment once we have unwittingly arrived at the place He needs us to be.

Ananias in Acts 9 is an example of just such a case of a divinely inspired and directed encounter. The first thing that stands out about Ananias is that Scripture says he was a disciple. He was not an apostle, prophet, pastor, or evangelist; he was simply a disciple. He does not appear to have been flamboyant or outgoing. In fact, he questioned God about the sincerity of Saul's intentions, showing his cautious nature. Being described as a disciple simply means that he was a devout follower of Jesus Christ and living his life intentionally with a heart for others. You may think I am reading something into the text that is not there, but it appears that this was the expectation of all believers in the first century. He was not only a disciple in name and title, but also in function.

Perhaps Ananias was at home when God spoke to him, but he was listening and willing to be a vessel of the Lord. God gave Ananias a vision of Saul of Tarsus. Does this indicate that Ananias had been praying and his mind and spirit were in tune with Christ and His mission to reach others? Why would God give a vision like this to someone who did not have a heart for others? In his vision, he saw Saul praying in Judas's house on the street called Straight, where he was waiting for Ananias to come and pray for him. Saul was also praying, and God gave him a vision of Ananias before he arrived at the house. When God has the attention of a praying disciple maker in one location and a potential disciple in range who is also reaching out for God, something special is going to happen.

This kind of divine appointment happened several times throughout the Book of Acts and other places in Scripture. God will give specific direction and order the steps of those who have committed themselves to making disciples. The Spirit led Philip into the desert on a disciple-making mission. He didn't have much time with his disciple, the Ethiopian eunuch, but he gave him a Bible study from Isaiah and then baptized him. This man apparently didn't need much discipling as he was already an ardent student of the Scriptures; he had come to Jerusalem to worship and perhaps was living a good life before the Lord. He simply needed some clarification and revelation concerning Christ and salvation. After the Bible study and subsequent revelation of his need for water baptism in the name of Jesus, Philip was instantly teleported many miles away.

We also have the example of Cornelius who was directed by God to send servants to Joppa to locate Simon the Tanner's house. Once there, they found Peter, who had received a vision and was subsequently directed to take the gospel to the Gentiles. This divine appointment led to the salvation of Cornelius's entire household and opened the door for the presentation of the gospel to the entire world.

However, not every divine appointment is so clearly directed. In fact, more often than not, God opens doors for making disciples when we are simply going through our daily lives with intentional hearts for others. For example, the Bible does not specifically say that Aquila and Priscilla were uniquely led by God the day they heard Apollos speaking in the synagogue. They apparently observed during his message that he was lacking revelation, so they took him aside and "explained the word of God more accurately to him" (Acts 18:26). Most ministry that happens beyond the walls of a house of worship occurs throughout daily routines. Peter and John were on the way to a prayer meeting when they served the need of the lame man who was healed.

Paul and Silas cast the devil out of a woman who followed them around but was entertaining a demonic spirit that inspired her to identify them as servants of the Most High God. Christian tradition contends that Paul's prison guards had to be changed often due to his persuasiveness in making disciples out of them. Paul was purposeful in his daily life. He said, "Therefore I run thus: not with uncertainty. Thus I fight: not as one who beats the air" (I Corinthians 9:26). Whether God supernaturally directs us to a specific person or if we simply take advantage of opportunities that present themselves during the routines of daily life, the key is to live purposefully and not randomly.

While Scripture records such events as the time that Jesus was "led by the Spirit into the wilderness" (Luke 4:1) and the time that He stated that He needed to go through Samaria, the majority of Jesus' disciple making occurred within the routine of every day. We should take note of this because He is our ultimate model and pattern. Consider how challenging it would be to relate to the New Testament model of making disciples if every action by the Lord and the apostles was preceded with, "And the Spirit told them to go talk to a certain man" or "And God spoke and gave them the address of the house where people were just waiting for someone to show up." Now don't get me wrong; amazing events like this happen to someone, somewhere, every day. But usually we just wake up, pray that God will direct our steps, and head out into the world with a disciple-maker's heart.

I first met one of my disciples within a few weeks after he moved into my neighborhood. When I noticed a dozen or so plainclothes and uniformed law enforcement officers closing in on his house across the street, it was a clue that maybe something serious was going on. It wasn't long until a SWAT vehicle pulled into his driveway, and over the loudspeaker ordered someone to come out of the house with her hands up. I found out later that his wife had suffered an emotional breakdown and had barricaded herself in the bathroom with a loaded weapon. She had threatened to harm herself and other family members. Within minutes the authorities deescalated the serious situation and took her away to a medical facility.

Within a few minutes, my wife and I met the husband on his doorstep with a smile and some freshly baked cookies. He seemed shook up to say the least, but our presence appeared to have a calming effect. I told him that I was a pastor, and we pledged our support to him and his children. I felt like the next move would be his, but it didn't happen for nearly two years. I would smile and wave when he was in his yard or driving by in his car, but nothing significant happened until one day as we were pulling in our driveway and he came running over to us. He asked some serious questions about life and relationships that I quickly directed to the Word of God. The next evening we began teaching him and his children a Bible study with life lessons mixed in. In fact, I spent two hours with them earlier today and just received a text message from him that said, "The lesson you taught tonight was great and my daughter and I were talking about it a long time after you left. We love having you in our lives."

That's disciple making. Disciple makers get into the lives of their disciples. Disciple makers are "there" intentionally and consistently, chatting in the front yard, hanging out for coffee, going to their kids' basketball games, and more.

Jesus said, "If you abide in Me, and My words abide in you, you will ask what you desire, and it shall be done for you. By this My Father is glorified, that you bear much fruit; so you will be My disciples" (John 15:7–8). Jesus didn't call them friends, associates, or children when He talked about fruitfulness, but he called them disciples. By using this term, He emphasized His relationship to them and their commitment to Him. How could His disciples better demonstrate that they were abiding in Christ and producing fruit that glorified God than when they were making disciples? Jesus also referred to the fruit associated with making disciples when He talked about fruit that will last in John 15:15, "You did not choose Me, but I chose you and appointed you that you should go and bear fruit, and that your fruit should remain, that whatever you ask the Father in My name He may give you." When we stay with our disciples as Jesus stayed with His disciples (John 17:12), the fruit of our discipleship will remain.

The vision of living an intentional life as modeled by Jesus was not intended to last only for one generation. The founder of the church prescribed exactly how He wanted His mission to be executed when He said, "Go make disciples." One full generation later, the apostle Paul wrote to Timothy and said, "And the things that you have heard from me among many witnesses, commit these to faithful men who will be able to teach others also" (II Timothy 2:2). Paul referenced the pattern demonstrated by Jesus as a sustainable method of reproducing the fruit of discipleship. Paul stressed the necessity of continuing in disciple-making relationships. He used words like *commit, teach*, and *faithful* along with the reference to his father-son relationship (in the gospel) with Timothy.

Jesus believed that His life was worth reproducing, and obviously Paul believed that his own life was worth reproducing, too. When he wrote to the Corinthians, he reminded them he was their spiritual father and said, "I urge you, imitate me" (I Corinthians 4:16). Then Paul said that he would be sending them Timothy, whose own behavior would remind them of his behavior. Later in the same letter, Paul stressed again the disciple-making pattern: "Follow me as I follow Christ" (I Corinthians 11:1, paraphrased).

It has been said that when we go to Heaven, the only thing we can take with us are the disciples that we make. While this is true, it is also true that the only thing we can leave behind are the disciples we make. Too many good Apostolic Christians are living like they are never going to die. They have not planned for their exit, they have no life insurance, and they have not made out a will or living trust. They have not given any directives about how they want their business taken care of. But more tragically, they are living for God like they will never die because they are not reproducing the fruit of their lives in others. When they are gone, there will be no trace of their precious lives here on earth. When we make disciples, we are making investments in others that will outlive us.

Many years ago, Bishop Morris Golder preached a now famous message titled, "The Interval Between." He said that on a tombstone there is a dash between the birth and death dates of the deceased. That dash is only about three inches long, but it represents everything that person has ever done in his or her lifetime. He emphasized that we have nothing to do with our birth date or death date, but everything to do with that interval between. Someone said that we are not in the land of the living going to the land of the dying, but we are in the land of the dying going to the land of the living. I can write a book, build a chair, paint a picture, or carve a bowl, but the only living thing that will outlive me are the people whose lives I have influenced. Jesus' disciples outlived Him and yours will too. Don't let your precious life come to a dead end when you're gone. Live every day intentionally!

Questions for discussion:

* What do you believe is the most significant accomplishment of your life to date?

* How would you describe the difference between going to church and being the church?

* In what ways can we live intentionally for others with a heart to make disciples out of them?

CHAPTER 4

DISCIPLE MAKING VERSUS SOULWINNING:

PENGUINS, NOT STORKS

In a previous chapter I presented the need to embrace proper theology before we can demonstrate authentic biblical practice. It then follows that improper theology will result in something less or other than biblical practice. With this understanding in mind I would like to turn our attention to the soulwinning language and practice that is commonly used in our Pentecostal culture.

Please do not think that I am against any effort employed to reach one person with the gospel. We fully understand and agree with Paul (I Corinthians 9:22) that by whatever means necessary, we must reach everyone we can with the saving message of Jesus Christ. I would suggest, however, that when church leaders speak about soulwinning, 90 percent of the congregation checks out for one of four reasons: (1) they don't do it (2) they don't relate to it (3) it doesn't fit their personality or gifting, or (4) they believe that only a few highly gifted people are called by God to do it. Too many soulwinning presentations attempt to goad good people into doing something beyond their perceived gifting or skill set. This is unfortunate because the problem is not with the congregation, but rather, with the limited paradigm of reaching the world that has been presented.

The bottom line is that most of the believers in our churches are intimidated by or unengaged with the soulwinning model we have perpetuated for generations. This cannot be the will of God. Is there something we can do to change the apathy or personal exemptions that saints give themselves about reaching lost people? I think there is something we can do if we will get back to what Jesus actually said, and not put words in His mouth.

Some would argue that apathy in church members toward reaching the world is a spiritual issue. The theory is, if we can get our people fasting and praying, then they will be inspired by God to go out and win the world. In some cases, it very well may be a spiritual issue, but I'm suggesting that there is more to the problem than that. I believe that not reaching people around us is a local church culture issue that can only be changed beginning at the top, but it can't be done overnight. People don't always do what the leader says, but they tend to do what the leader does. However, this is only the beginning of "fixing" the reluctance of members in our local churches to labor for the harvest.

Every local congregation has a culture, whether it is intended or not. The culture of the local church is largely inspired by the vision, preaching, teaching, communicating (verbal and nonverbal), and attitude of the pastor. Whatever he or she is, the congregation will become. J. T. Pugh said, "Whatever is in the heart of the pastor will come out in the congregation." If the pastor is modeling a heart for lost people, not by just preaching sermons about the harvest, but actually modeling that practice, then that is a good start toward changing the local church culture.

I discovered a long time ago that I cannot change the church I serve from behind the pulpit. The only way I can change the culture of the church I lead is to model the practice I want to see reproduced in the members of the congregation. I must come out of my office, step out from behind the pulpit, and come down from the platform to interact with people up close. This was Jesus' method of creating a disciple-making culture. He didn't just preach to the masses, but He intentionally spent time with people, one-on-one, making disciples who then turned around and made more disciples.

In my view, pastors need to think long and hard about the culture they desire to embed within the congregations they are serving. There are basically two ways to motivate and inspire the people we lead to reach the people around them: program-based evangelism or Bible-based disciple making. The majority of what our movement has done historically to reach lost people has been based around programs designed to attract new people to the church. Programs can serve a purpose or a mission but they often fall short of making a lasting impact on the people they are designed to reach.

What usually happens is that we measure the success of a program by how many people showed up rather than the difference it made in the participants. Much of what we have done to reach lost people has been based around events such as block parties, special occasion Sundays, door-knocking campaigns, street services, and other cold-turkey evangelistic initiatives.

I am not disparaging any of these endeavors. In fact, I have participated in all of them and more through the years, both as a saint and a pastor. But there is a better and more biblical way to impact lost people. I would go so far as to suggest that if we would have engaged the biblical method of reaching the world (the first-century method) we might have reached the whole world by now.

Maybe someone reading this is thinking, "Aren't soulwinning and disciple making the same thing?" My response is they are not the same thing, at least not in the way we have traditionally understood them. Many people think that soulwinning is the effort that brings people to obedience of the gospel, and disciple making is the aspect that establishes them in the church. To the credit of some, if they have any concept at all of disciple making, then they are much further down the road than most. Unfortunately, many have a sense that once we introduce sinners to the new-birth message and they are born again, then our work is done. However, the truth is that the heavy lifting of disciple making begins after the new birth. Salvation is not a diploma but a birth certificate. I would suggest that reaching the world with the gospel of Christ is the mission of the church but the biblically prescribed method to accomplish this commission of Christ is not to win souls but to make disciples.

If soulwinning is like a microwave, then disciple making is like a Crock-Pot. This is why Jesus told us to go make disciples. Think about it: After you "win" then what? When you win it's over, but when you make disciples the process is ongoing. Regardless of the theological implications, you can see the difference that terminology makes when communicating the mission of the church. Jesus did not tell us to win anything, but rather to go make everything.

Winning communicates a short, measurable sequence of time after which there is no more obligation, but *making* communicates a skillful, labor-intensive, open-ended season of personal investment and oversight. When a local congregation has a soulwinning mentality, their retention rate will be predictably low, but when they possess a disciple-making vision, their retention rate will be significantly higher. In a typical year of reaching lost people through soulwinning strategies, our local retention rate was around 15 percent. Once we changed our missional paradigm to disciple making, our retention rate jumped dramatically to 71 percent. Reaching lost people should never be reduced to a numbers game. We should not be thinking that we need to baptize x number of people so that we can retain or grow by y number of people. One pastor stated that his church needed to baptize hundreds to keep fifty. I think there's something wrong with this approach. Jesus said that He had lost none of His disciples because He stayed with them (John 17:12). The power of making disciples is staying with your disciples. It slows down the journey, but how much better for two to cross the finish line together than just one alone?

There are problems with some terms we use when talking about reaching lost people. Let's take a look at the word *evangelism*. I would suggest that evangelism is not what the early church did. Evangelism is one of the fivefold ministries. (See Ephesians 4:11.) God-called evangelists have the passion and ability to quickly and consistently bring sinners to a decision to follow Jesus Christ and lead them into the obedience of His gospel. They have the God-given gifting to do this from behind a pulpit or one-on-one. We should take note, however, that *evangelism* or *evangelize* is never used in the Scriptures and that the word *evangelist* is used only three times. Jesus did not say, "Go evangelize the world."

I agree that soulwinning certainly has something to do with the Great Commission as we have defined it, but the hard truth is that this is not what Jesus told us to do. The good news is that making disciples is the correct biblical language that describes the method Christ directed us to use to reach the world, one at a time, from the spiritual cradle to the grave (or rapture). It has often been said that we don't go to church two or three times per week, but we are the church everywhere we go. By the same token, evangelism is something that we may do on Saturday visitation, street service, block parties, or other such endeavors, but disciple makers is what we are, everywhere we go, 24/7.

When we talk about soulwinning we are talking about reaching lost people with the only saving gospel of Jesus Christ. This vision is not only compelling but also necessary because reaching the lost is the only way to expand the kingdom of God. However, I would suggest that the term *soulwinning* is somewhat problematic for a few reasons: (1) it is not what Jesus told us to do, (2) it is not New Testament language, (3) very few within local congregations relate to it, (4) it is not usually associated with making disciples, (5) it is often presented and received with a high dose of guilt-motivation, (6) it is not how we live our daily lives, (7) it is usually presented within a program or an unnatural institutionalized context.

Making disciples is not just about what happens after a sinner is saved, but it accurately describes the journey from the first contact with an undiscipled person to the last step in Heaven with Christ and the church. Jesus did not compartmentalize new birth and spiritual maturity. He placed it all under one grand vision of making disciples.

As Oneness Pentecostals, we believe that the first-century brand of Christianity is who we are. We have a strong restorationist impulse among us that compels us back to the beginning of the church that started in Jerusalem. Those first-century Christians experienced the full gospel of Jesus Christ by repenting of their sins, receiving water baptism in the name of Jesus, and being filled with the Holy Spirit initially evidenced by speaking with other tongues. Although our definition of Christian initiation has been gaining traction around the world, contending for it creates a stir of opposition with others who consider themselves to be Christians, but do not agree with us.

When we add to our definition of Christianity the revelation of the Mighty God in Christ; the fivefold ministry; the full operation of the gifts of the Spirit; the working of miracles, wonders, and signs; and inward and outward marks of devotion that separate us from the world, then we further distance ourselves from the pack. However, before we celebrate our full revelation and obedience to full New Testament Christianity, I'm suggesting there is one thing we yet lack.

There is at least one more characteristic that was embedded in the first-century culture of Christians and that is they all understood their mission was to go make disciples. We somehow do not understand this. Our practice reveals what we think about Jesus' command to go make disciples. We simply don't do it, but we think it is getting done. We send missionaries overseas, North American missionaries to unchurched cities, youth groups to go on missions trips around the world, and we gladly celebrate the super-spiritual and outgoing personality types among us who evangelize our local communities, but a majority of the average local church does not typically fulfill the Great Commission.

We are faithful to church, pay our tithes, sing in the choir, and maybe even go out of our way occasionally to shake the guests' hands in our local church, but we forget their names before church is over, much less have a plan to be intentional and make a disciple out of them. Jesus didn't tell us to procure a building and hang a sign out front that says, "Y'all come." I don't think we can say we have fulfilled the Great Commission by simply having visitors show up. We have an obligation after they leave to follow up and make disciples.

Jesus did not tell us to go win souls. He certainly could have told us to go win souls. But is soulwinning what He really meant when He said to "go make disciples"? I don't think so. There are reasons why Jesus said "go make disciples" and not "go win souls." Consider the origin of the idea of soulwinning: Proverbs 11:30 says, "The fruit of the righteous is a tree of life. And he who wins souls is wise." First, this text is situated in the Old Testament. Second, notice the context of this verse. Does the context involve leading someone to God or to salvation? Most likely not. The most we can deduce from the context is that it takes wisdom to make friends. The New Living Translation renders this phrase from Proverbs 11:30, "A wise person wins friends." Without reading evangelism into the text, one would be hard-pressed to use this as a text to describe how we win people to a conversion experience with God. In fact, conversion was not a main focus in the Old Testament, nor did it appear to have been the primary mission of God's people.

Let's make a quick comparison of a soulwinner versus a disciple maker and observe which one has a more far-reaching impact. Let's say that there is a gifted soulwinner who has the skills, personality, and anointing to win one soul per day. There are people in some of our churches who are equipped to do this. Needless to say, this kind of a ministry is impressive. So let's say that a soulwinner wins one soul per day for an entire year. At the end of that year, that person would have won 365 souls. How exciting is that?

This kind of soulwinning success would be celebrated all over the world. This person would be called upon to conduct seminars from sea to shining sea. But now here is the question: You say you won souls, but did you make any disciples? Are any of those people walking with God now? Are they participating in a local congregation? Have they turned around and begun making disciples with their friends? The answer to these questions may be, "We don't know," or "Probably not." And let's say that this soulwinner won one soul a day not just for a year but for thirty years. That would be 10,950 born-again people. But once again, do we have any disciples? Are they committed to a local congregation and engaged in making disciples? We don't know for sure but most likely they are not.

Now let's take a look at the disciple maker. Let's say that this person takes an entire year to fully disciple and establish one lost person. During that year, the disciple maker spends weekly time with his or her disciple, leads that person to a new-birth experience, and teaches him or her the essential doctrines of the Bible. Emphasis is given to walking with God daily, sharing his or her testimony with friends and family, and the importance of having a pastor and joining a local congregation, with the expectation that the one being discipled will become a disciple maker.

At the end of that first year there is only the disciple maker and the disciple. And after the second year, there are only two disciple makers and two disciples. But after thirty years we would have one billion disciples. According to author Talmadge French there are 15–20 million Oneness Pentecostals in the world today (French 1999, 17). Using the formula of a disciple making one disciple per year, the Apostolic church could theoretically disciple the entire world's population in nine years.

If you know the difference between a stork and a penguin, then you know the difference between evangelizing people and discipling people. Hans Christian Andersen wrote a fanciful tale about storks bringing newborn babies to their awaiting families. It is believed that the myth of the stork delivering babies was invented by adults who didn't want to explain to their children where babies come from. Unfortunately, some local congregations have adopted the mythology of the stork as their concept of discipleship: the stork picks up the baby in a huge diaper, flies that baby to the right address, rings the doorbell with its beak, and then flies away. Too many congregations have no plan to make disciples, assuming that when people get saved, God flips the autopilot switch inside of them and they become saints all by themselves.

I am suggesting that we need to be less like storks and more like penguins when it comes to developing spiritual maturity in new believers. Emperor penguins breed during the cold Antarctic winter and lay their eggs in May. After the female lays her egg she passes it off to the male. He keeps the egg warm by tucking it under a pouch of skin just under his belly and above his feet. He balances the egg there for sixty-four days during which time the female travels to the ocean to hunt.

The male huddles with other males in the colony while they help to keep each other warm. They fast the entire time and incubate their eggs faithfully until the return of their female counterparts. The females return around the time that the egg hatches with a belly full of food to feed their young. They take over caring for their hatchlings, regurgitating the food they caught while the males travel to the ocean for their first meal in more than one hundred days.

For the next fifty days, the parents continually switch back and forth; one hunts while the other stays to feed the chick. When the chick is about two months old it starts spending more time away from its parents, though it still depends on them for food. The parents leave them in a group of chicks called a crèche that is supervised by other penguins in the colony. They can now go hunting together, but this hunt is not as time consuming because the warm spring weather brings the shoreline closer to the colony's nesting site. When the parents return to the colony, they reunite with their chick to feed them.

After a Saturday men's prayer breakfast, I was asked by one of our relatively new believers if he could talk to me in my office. He had no idea what I was going to preach to the congregation the next day. I had said nothing to anyone about it. During the message I was going to use the illustration I just shared about storks versus penguins. While we were in my office visiting, the Holy Ghost spoke to him three times to tell me that he needed a penguin. He argued with the Lord, "I'm not going to tell my pastor I need a penguin. He will think I'm crazy." He said nothing to me about it in our meeting. During my message the next day, he was going crazy inside as he listened to me share the need for penguins in the church. He was excited to know that not only was he hearing the voice of God, but God was revealing a need in his life.

In my personal experience of making disciples I have always taken the Crock-Pot approach. If I can get my foot in someone's door and to their kitchen table with a Bible study, I will drag it out as long as I can. My intention is to give my disciples an opportunity to "buy in" to me as a Christian and a man of God. I have found that authentic Apostolic Christianity will shine through easily if you are given several opportunities to sit down and present the Word of God for an hour or two at a time.

I make disciples out of my Bible study students without them even realizing it. I am currently making a disciple of my neighbor who literally lives across the street from me. I've been in his house once a week for eight months. He has not been to our church one time nor have I invited him. He had "religion" shoved down his throat as a kid growing up in the projects. He witnessed gross hypocrisy and therefore has been turned off by "religious" people. He told me recently that he is now "very biased" toward me and my approach to teaching him and his children the Word of God. He holds every other pastor or preacher he knows or hears accountable to my standard. He has not been born again yet, but one day he will want to be saved and he will know what to do and where to go to get it done. I will not leave him until this happens. A stork doesn't come to his doorstep every Tuesday at 4:00 PM and ring the doorbell, but a penguin does.

Questions for discussion:

- What are some differences between soulwinning and disciple making?

- Do you think there are differences between how the first-century church lived their personal lives and how we live ours regarding reaching lost people?

- What are some things that you can do to incorporate the idea of being more like a penguin than a stork as a disciple maker?

CHAPTER 5

FOLLOW TO LEAD:
THE GAME CHANGER

Where did Jesus discover His model of making disciples? As we discussed earlier, Jesus did not employ any of the measures that are often used today to plant and grow a church. He mailed no flyers, He wrote no letters, He took out no billboards, nor did He write a book to gain popularity. He did not do any of the things that are typically done today to gain prominence within a community. So where did He get His game plan to change the world?

Jesus did not come up with anything new as a method to reach the world with His message. He did something sustainable and reproducible in any culture and any generation. He used the disciple-making culture that was already ensconced in the mindset of His Jewish culture. Why reinvent the wheel? It is likely that nothing will ever be more effective in reaching the world than disciple making. While it is true that disciple making was culturally normative in first-century Galilee and Judea, other experiences may have influenced Jesus' methodology. Could John the Baptist have been one of those influences? He certainly was the one who prepared the way for Jesus. There are several similar patterns in their overlapping ministries. We know that their mothers were cousins. We know that John was six months older, a Levite, and the son of a priest. Jesus, on the other hand, grew up in the home of a carpenter.

His episode in the Temple with the doctors of the Law at the age of twelve gives us insight into the fact that early on He was focused, intense, and aware of His mission. To the amazement of His parents, the events of that day clearly identified Jesus as rabbi material and that He definitely was not destined for a career in carpentry.

John and Jesus both came out of the wilderness to launch their ministries. It is remarkable that John made disciples within a short time who were loyal to him and his message. In fact, Paul discovered disciples of John some twenty years after his beheading, and found them to be yet following in the footsteps of their Rabbi (Acts 19:1–6).

Jesus' disciples also lasted beyond the life of their short-lived Rabbi, and they endured to the end as they eventually all died in the faith. Rabbis did not commonly baptize their disciples, but John baptized his disciples, as did Jesus. John introduced Jesus to the world as was the privilege of every rabbi to introduce his disciples. John said that Jesus must increase and he himself must decrease (the true spirit of a rabbi desiring his student to exceed him in every way). Jesus told His disciples that they would do greater things than He. We typically do not think of Jesus having a rabbi or mentor in His life, but from a human standpoint, it is entirely possible that John had some early influence on the practice and ministry of the Christ.

Other places in Scripture demonstrate elements of the rabbi-disciple motif. When Elijah was caught up in a horse-drawn chariot of fire, he dropped his mantle upon Elisha. Elisha went straight to the river he had just miraculously passed through with his rabbi and performed the exact same action. He smote the water and cried out, "Where is the LORD God of Elijah?" (II Kings 2:14). We might say that Elisha was imitating his rabbi.

What explosive growth every local church would experience if every believer made one disciple per year. But there is something even more dynamic than that. What if every disciple maker stayed with that disciple until each one in turn began to make a disciple? The endgame of being a Christian in the first century was more than just to bring others to faith in Christ. Their pattern took discipling one step further by modeling Christlike practice alongside disciples until they themselves began to make disciples.

Reproducing ourselves in others is undoubtedly the ultimate goal and demonstration of full maturity in Christ. We see the model of spiritual reproduction unfold in the Book of Acts and throughout the epistles. Paul said, "Imitate me just as I also imitate Christ" (I Corinthians 11:1). John wrote, "I have no greater joy than to hear that my children walk in truth" (III John 4). Peter wrote that Christ left a model so that you should follow His steps (I Peter 2:21). In Acts 8:4 the believers went everywhere preaching the Word and were accused by their detractors as these that have turned the world upside down. Ananias and Barnabas teamed up to make a disciple out of Saul of Tarsus (Acts 9–13). Aquila and Priscilla took Apollos aside and explained the way of God more accurately (Acts 18:26). New believers or underdeveloped Christians were nurtured by leaders and mature believers in hopes of developing their maturity in Christ.

The evidence of true discipleship or maturity in Christ is fruitfulness. When Jesus talked to the disciples about being fruitful in John 15 He said that He was the vine and they were the branches. He let them know that without Him they could do nothing and that their connectedness to the vine was the prerequisite to becoming fruitful. There are many ways that mature believers can become fruitful. The most obvious fruit we can bear is the fruit of the Spirit (Galatians 5:22-23). We can also bear the fruit of the gifts of the Spirit (I Corinthians 12:7-10).

As we mature in Christ we will become faithful to God's house; schedule daily prayer and time in the Word; begin to demonstrate the character, nature, and attitude of Christ; begin to return our tithe to the Lord and give offerings; and get involved in local church ministries. There is not a pastor in the world who would not love to have a congregation of believers manifesting the fruit that has just been described. I would suggest, however, there is more fruit to bear.

Consider that the maturity described above is actually the fruit of Christ in us. The radical change and spiritual development within us is the fruitfulness of Jesus in us, but what is the fruit of your life in others? No matter how spiritual we are, we cannot give anyone the fruit of the Spirit. I cannot give anyone patience, gentleness, peace, love, joy, or any other Christlike characteristics. These are the character traits that Christ manifests in us through the power of His Word and the Holy Spirit. These practices and attributes are the manifestation of His fruit in us. In John 15 Jesus placed a demand of fruitfulness upon us. So if the fruit of my life is to be demonstrated in some tangible way, and if I cannot personally give or reproduce within anyone the fruit of Christ that is manifested in me, then what fruit can I bear?

I believe that the fruitfulness Jesus was talking about in John 15 also involves the fruitfulness of making disciples. Jesus employed the metaphor of the vine, the branch, and the fruit. The ultimate goal of being fruitful is to reproduce. Contained within every living thing is the ability to reproduce itself. Without the ability to reproduce, any species will become extinct within one generation.

Every fruit reproduces another perfect specimen exactly like itself. I think it should be obvious to us that our fruitfulness is not what we do at church or a godly character trait or spiritual gift, but our fruitfulness is to reproduce after our kind, to make another one just like us. Whether or not you agree with this interpretation of fruitfulness, it remains that at least some aspect of Jesus placing a demand of fruitfulness and reproduction on us has something to do with making disciples.

Making disciples should be as natural as a grape reproducing grapes or a husband and wife reproducing children. Disciples are being made every day all over this world, but for other purposes: drug dealers are making disciples, pornographers are making disciples, rock stars are making disciples, extreme Islamists are making disciples, and even marketers in corporate America are making disciples. Making disciples seems to be a natural by-product of all these aberrant and heretical groups, so why shouldn't disciple making be as natural for us as going to church, reading the Word, and lifting our hands and worshiping our great God? The church must rise up and counter all the anti-God and anti-biblical disciple making by reproducing biblical values, principles, and practices in our disciples.

I am convinced that Apostolics today embrace the new birth, doctrine, and lifestyle (in terms of holiness and separation) of the first-century church. However, I am not as sure that we live our lives on a daily basis as they did when it comes to being fruitful in making disciples. There is a significant difference in being a Christian by today's definition and being a disciple by the first-century definition. The endgame of being a disciple in the first century was to become a disciple maker. This is a much different picture than what being a Christian is today.

There is little expectation placed on new believers regarding the making of disciples. Most pastors are happy to have their new converts coming to church at least once a week, and anything they might do for God beyond that is a bonus. Other pastors are satisfied if their new believers become established and stop smoking, stop cursing, take off their jewelry, sing in the choir, and pay their tithes.

Herein lies the problem and perhaps is one reason for our lack of having a greater impact in our communities. A changed life is wonderful and one of the great benefits of obeying the gospel, but we must begin to build within a local church culture the expectation that new believers quickly turn around and make disciples (and not wait for years until their ship of full spiritual maturity comes in).

Americans love choices and options, but Proverbs 22:6 instructs parents to "train up a child in the way he should go and when he is old he will not depart from it." This language carries the idea of the parents placing the correct choices within their child. The word *train* means to "narrow," "initiate," or "disciple" (the word *depart* means "to turn off"). As a pastor I have often taken the word *train* and used the illustration of a train on a track. The child is the train and parenting is the track. Good parenting, early in a child's life, establishes the character that will help them to make the right choices in order to keep them on the right track.

Some behavioral psychologists suggest that a child's character is formed by his or her seventh birthday. The lesson for pastors and the local church is that we need to teach, train, demonstrate, and model disciple-making behavior in our new believers immediately after their new birth. One old-time preacher was approached by a young mother who wanted to know how old her only child should be before she began to teach him the Word of God. He asked her how old the child was. When she replied "seven" he said, "Hurry home, woman, you're seven years too late."

There is no such thing as a "revival lottery." There are no special formulas, secrets, or shortcuts to growth in a local church. If you are truly growing the kingdom of God by making disciples, then I can tell you it is plain, old-fashioned hard work. Have you ever wondered what the real reason was for the explosive growth in the first-century church? I marvel at it every time I read the text. The upper room started out with 120, then later that day three thousand more were added to the Lord, then five thousand (Acts 4:4), and then multitudes. Believers were "added" to the church (Acts 2:41, 47) and the number of disciples was "multiplied" (Acts 6:1, 7).

Perhaps Luke was recalling the numbers associated with conversions, but when the estimated total exceeded five thousand, he simply referred to a massive multiplication of disciples, which infers a number well above five thousand. How did the church go from addition to multiplication? Did they plan large group events? Crusades? Block parties? The Day of Pentecost outpouring was certainly a factor, but that event was divinely orchestrated and unplanned by the disciples. It appears to me that the exponential growth of the early church was made possible because born-again believers were aggressively engaged in the daily process of making disciples.

We know that personal disciple making was the model Jesus gave His followers to reach the world, and according to the Book of Acts it worked well. But when did Jesus' expectation of them not just to follow Him but to turn around and lead others begin to sink in? When did it dawn on the twelve disciples as they followed Jesus that they were not following just to follow?

I'm sure early on in their association with Jesus that they felt rather privileged. Let's be honest; they had every reason to feel special. After all, they had been carefully and personally chosen by the Lord Himself out of a group of hundreds who would have jumped at the chance. After Jesus taught a particular multitude, as He and His disciples left their adoring onlookers and journeyed to the next town, did the disciples wave to the spectators like Super Bowl champions walking off the field?

The Twelve had a sideline seat for every word, action, and miracle performed by their Rabbi. When Jesus was invited to dinners, weddings, and other special occasions, it was understood that they would accompany Him. Wow, what a meal ticket! This was too good to be true. Lowly fishermen, tax collectors, and zealots were secured in an entourage of the man who appeared to be able to overthrow the Romans and take back their beloved homeland. Jesus was their Moses leading them to the Promised Land and they were along for the ride.

In John 1 Jesus amazed Nathaniel when He informed him that He saw him under the fig tree just prior to their meeting. Nathaniel might have been a little embarrassed when it dawned on him that if Jesus supernaturally saw him under the fig tree, then He probably heard what he said about Him too: "Can anything good come out of Nazareth?" (John 1:46). Jesus told Nathaniel in verse 50, "You will see greater things than these." Now that sounded really good. But it wasn't long until Jesus was not only saying that they would see greater things than these, but He began to say, "Most assuredly, I say to you, he who believes in Me, the works that I do he will do also; and greater works than these he will do, because I go to My Father" (John 14:12).

Jesus began to steadily ramp up His expectations of His disciples. He not only told them they would eventually be doing what He was doing, but He sent them out to do it. Luke 10 is probably the moment that it hit them they were in training to do the things Jesus had been doing alone up to this point.

This was the game changer for the disciples. They realized that they were not following just to follow, but Jesus' plan for them was to follow for now, but eventually lead. Follow to lead: This simple concept is the reason for the dramatic growth in the first-century church. I've known pastors that wanted to attract all the followers they could but didn't want any leaders. This mentality keeps churches small and stunts the growth of saints. In fact, leaders will not be attracted to a church that does not have a track for leadership development and opportunities to lead.

When you have a follower you have the power of one, but if you have a leader you have the power of exponential growth. If there was any secret to the success of the first-century church in terms of the impact on Jerusalem, Judea, Samaria, and the uttermost part of the earth, it was their expectation of a disciple. They believed that a disciple was one who followed to lead, not one who got saved, came to church, and nodded in approval as the pastor went through the liturgy.

Mature believers would do well to replicate this first-century disciple-making behavior. Any pastor would covet a disciple-making culture within his or her congregation. Such a culture develops deeper spiritual maturity in the saints while reproducing their qualities in the lives of new believers. The essential element from day one is to immediately communicate to young disciples that the actions, attitudes, commitment, and oversight provided for them must soon become their lifestyles and that in turn, they begin to make the same investment in their disciples. Paul placed this demand on his disciple Timothy when he wrote, "And the things that you have heard from me among many witnesses, commit these to faithful men who will be able to teach others also" (II Timothy 2:2).

Questions for discussion:

- Who do you know that you would describe as being effective in reproducing themselves in others?

- What challenges does Western culture present in establishing a disciple-making culture in a local church?

- Where has the church generally fallen short with the development of new believers?

- How would you rate your fruitfulness?

CHAPTER 6

STRAIGHT TALK TO PASTORS ABOUT MAKING DISCIPLES:

THE PRICE
OF DISCIPLESHIP IS HIGH

I would suggest that most pastors, including myself, have been too easygoing on the members of our congregations when it comes to assigning them the responsibility of making disciples. In what tradition might our reluctance be rooted? Have we unwittingly perpetuated a myth that only people possessing certain personality types, skill sets, or the gift of evangelism are capable of making disciples? If so, this may be one of the reasons that we have not had a greater impact on our communities and the world.

The bar of expectations has been set far too low in the area of making disciples. Our problem is two-fold: Who do we qualify to make disciples and what expectations do we place on our new believers once they become born again? I believe that for too long our subconscious goal has been to get people saved, and see them paying their tithes and coming to church three times a week. This profile of a twenty-first-century believer is much different than that of a first-century disciple.

We need to take a long hard look at how we are doing the business of the Great Commission. If we have not yet caught the method of the mission prescribed by the Founder, then it follows that we have not challenged or equipped our congregations to go make disciples. As a limited substitute we have employed every motivational mechanism imaginable in an attempt to engage our saints in reaching lost people including door knocking, street services, block parties, mass mailings, and other special event days. Such efforts have netted results to be sure, but none of these efforts are organic or naturally sustainable, and they do not capture the essence of how we live our lives every day. Some have even employed tactics such as guilt, fear, intimidation, and even manipulation in their desperate attempt to engage faithful church members in the harvest. This is not what Jesus had in mind when He said to go make disciples.

We should reconsider our thinking about the responsibility that has been tasked to the members of our congregations to go make disciples. Perhaps we should reevaluate our approach and get biblically honest with our good and faithful church members about what Christ expects them to do with their lives. I have found that most of the saints I lead want to live up to the expectations I place on them as their pastor, not to mention what they would want to do for Christ. Pastors communicate their expectations to the members of their assemblies by how they preach to them and speak with them personally, and by the practice they model before them. If the expectation is for saints to just come to church, sing in the choir, come to prayer meeting, and give in the offering, then that is exactly what pastors will get. However, if the expectation is that they will go and make a disciple this year, I believe that most of them will respond positively.

Jesus didn't just preach great messages and teach profound truths to His disciples on Sundays and Wednesdays. His goal was not to be popular or for them to like Him. He was not satisfied by drawing a big crowd, working a few miracles, feeding them, and sending them home with a warm feeling in their hearts. He placed a demand on His disciples to reproduce the same disciple-making practice He had demonstrated with them.

Some pastors may hesitate to place a strong expectation of making disciples on individual members of their congregations. Their reluctance to deliver the biblical mandate given to all believers may be rooted in apathy, a fear of rejection, or a concern that members might transfer to another church where less commitment is expected. There are a few biblical subjects that we pastors are sometimes hesitant to teach and preach. One of them is the biblical approach to financial stewardship. The classic fear is that someone in the congregation will interpret the presentation on tithing as an attempt by pastors to line their own pockets.

The truth is that if we neglect to teach financial stewardship then not only are we circumventing our responsibility but we are also denying ignorantly disobedient members in our congregations the opportunity to live a financially blessed life. The same could be said of the mandate to make disciples; there is no greater joy in the world than taking responsibility to facilitate the spiritual birth and maturity of others. I certainly am not suggesting that we become tyrannical in our approach to casting the vision of making disciples, but neither should we shrink back from it. There is a way to engage our congregations to joyfully rise up and receive the challenge delivered by Christ to go make disciples.

Christ's call to go make disciples is not for the faint of heart. Right from the start it is possible to either qualify or not qualify at being His disciple. Jesus placed expectations upon His disciples. In fact, you could say that He was intense about the qualifications He required. He was the greatest speaker, motivator, and recruiter the world has ever seen. But unlike some leaders who attempt to get a new company or venture off the ground, Jesus did not use bait-and-switch tactics. He did not offer special discounts for those who responded first or extra perks for ground-level applicants. He did not sneak up on people and try to soft sell His vision. He used straight talk. One thing I've always appreciated about the way Jesus communicated was that He personally modeled commitment before He preached commitment or asked for commitment.

John 6 records the narrative for the feeding of the five thousand. He gave this enormous gathering a "dinner and a show." But that's when the free stuff stopped. I wonder what might have been going through the disciples' minds when Jesus started speaking. His message certainly wasn't of the feel-good sort popularized by some TV evangelists. Apparently He was not making His message palatable enough so that the uncommitted would want to come back next week for more of the same.

Some of His disciples might have wished Jesus had attended a Dale Carnegie seminar before He gave this message. His comments sure didn't seem like a good way to build a massive following. Instead of a warm and fuzzy presentation, Jesus spoke directly to the heart of what He was offering:

> Most assuredly, I say to you, unless you eat the flesh of the Son of Man and drink His blood, you have no life in you. Whoever eats My flesh and drinks My blood has eternal life, and I will raise him up at the last day. For My flesh is food indeed, and My blood is drink indeed. He who eats My flesh and drinks My blood abides in Me, and I in him. As the living Father sent Me, and I live because of the Father, so he who feeds on Me will live because of Me. This is the bread which came down from heaven—not as your fathers ate the manna, and are dead. He who eats this bread will live forever. (John 6:53–58)

Notice the reaction to His call to commitment: "Therefore many of His disciples, when they heard this, said, 'This is a hard saying; who can understand it?' When Jesus knew in Himself that His disciples complained about this, He said to them, 'Does this offend you?' . . . From that time many of His disciples went back and walked with Him no more" (John 6:60–61, 66). Here is what Jesus understood about His mission and the kind of people He needed to get the job done: until He preached commitment He would never know who was in His audience.

When we as pastors fail to preach commitment, we are doing Christ, the mission, ourselves, and our audience a disservice. Without asking for a commitment from the multitude we will never build a congregation. I have yet to lose a committed person because

I preached commitment. When I preach about giving, givers don't get upset and quit. When I preach about having a daily prayer life, the people who pray don't stop coming to church. When we preach commitment, we may lose some from the crowd, but at least we choose who we lose. Jesus lost people and we will too if we follow His model of placing a demand on our followers. But we will not lose true disciples. And if they are not going to commit to being disciples who follow, and they leave, what have we lost?

One reason an Apostolic church does not grow as fast as some other churches could be because we preach and expect commitment. This is not an excuse for lack of growth, but it is our reality. It costs something to be a part of a church that teaches the full gospel of repentance and baptism of water and Spirit. That alone is enough to turn off people who believe they are saved by repeating the sinner's prayer. It costs something to be part of a congregation that teaches and models a separated lifestyle from the world. Separation from the world is a clear and time-less scriptural doctrine, but it is not "culturally correct" today. Apostolic churches have a spirit of holiness about them that carries a spirit of conviction. People who don't want to change their lifestyles and carnal ways turn back at the moment of conviction, and like those in John 6, walk with Him no more. Apostolic churches expect their members to plan their calendars around the house of God and be there and participate when ministry is going on. They expect their members to dedicate time, talent, and treasure to the mission of Christ. But there is one thing we yet lack: it is time to cast the vision, equip every member of our congregation, and place an expectation on them to go make disciples.

We must come to grips with the first-century model and expectations of being a disciple. Too many twenty-first-century Apostolic believers fall short of Jesus' job description to be His follower. Part of the reason we miss the message of discipleship is because of cultural differences, but the essence and expectation must not be lost. There is a price to pay for being a disciple of Jesus Christ. That price begins with coming out of the world and giving up sin, addictions, and practices that would only condemn us in eternity anyway. But the real price begins to be paid when we initiate interaction with others who need salvation through Christ and invest our literal lives in their spiritual journey.

It is easier to travel alone without being burdened by the added weight of the disciple(s) we are carrying. We can journey much faster alone without having to wait for new believers to catch up with all the baggage they carry. Making disciples on the road to Heaven is not the easy way, and it slows our progress, yet this is the pace that Jesus called us to embrace. Disciples make disciples, so be sure that you are taking the journey with someone.

Jesus didn't pull any punches when He began speaking to that first-century Jewish population about what it would cost to follow Him:

> And when Jesus saw great multitudes about Him, He gave a command to depart to the other side. Then a certain scribe came and said to Him, "Teacher, I will follow You wherever You go." And Jesus said to him, "Foxes have holes and birds of the air have nests, but the Son of Man has nowhere to lay His head." Then another of His disciples

said to Him, "Lord, let me first go and
bury my father." But Jesus said to him,
"Follow Me, and let the dead bury their
own dead." (Matthew 8:18–22)

Jesus didn't coddle or cajole, He just spoke plainly
about the cost of discipleship.

The core idea of Christianity is not to be a church
member but to be a Christ follower. What does it mean
to be a Christ follower? It means to pattern your life
after the life of the historic man named Jesus Christ.
The problem with pop Christianity is the temptation
to cherry-pick what is desirable about Jesus' example
and ignore the rest. Apostolic Christians can be equally
guilty of the same. We love His person, His deity, His
attitude, His presence, and His passion, but the vast
majority are doing absolutely nothing to make disciples.
Some Christians are out of balance because they are
quite comfortable with hand-picked aspects of the
demands of Christ but don't seem to be interested in
other weightier matters.

A lack of true discipleship produces followers who
are out of balance and unhealthy. This would be somewhat like a body builder who only works out the right
side of his body. How strange it would be to see a
21-inch bicep on one side of the body and an 8-inch
bicep on the other. To follow the analogy even further,
someone asked a weightlifter what he did with all those
muscles. He immediately went into a typical weightlifter
pose and flexed. The person asking the question was
exasperated but tried again, "No, I mean what do you
do with all of those muscles?" The weightlifter smiled
and went into another pose and flexed again. That's
about right: We pose and flex our Pentecostal power

to worship and preach on Sunday but do nothing to make disciples Monday through Saturday.

It is popular in Christianity today to take seriously the words of Christ in Matthew 5–7 and live out the Beatitudes by feeding the hungry, turning the other cheek, going the second mile, and giving our coat. All of these commands are important, but this list does not include the most important message from Jesus Christ to us. Some Christian groups try to make you feel as though you're not doing anything for God unless you're passing out water, food, and clothing, and digging wells in third-world countries. We thank God for all that has been done to promote social justice. Humanitarian efforts are beneficial, but a social gospel will never save anyone. These efforts may make people more physically comfortable, and possibly even open a door to their most important need—receiving the saving gospel of Jesus Christ—but doing these things was not the primary message of Jesus Christ. The priority of Jesus was the lost world He came to save. He didn't come to this earth to feed, clothe, and heal the world. John the Baptist said the Messiah's primary ministry would be to baptize with the Holy Ghost and fire (Matthew 3:11). Jesus' priority was to seek and to save the lost. His method to do so was to make disciples out of sinners and friends (Matthew 11:19).

So what was the priority for Jesus' followers? What did He want them to take away from His time here on earth? His priority was for His followers to become His disciples and then for them to turn around and make disciples. Jesus has called us to be His disciples by following Him, and therefore He has sent us to go and make disciples. We follow to lead.

Christ-prescribed discipleship may cost you time, emotion, physical energy, money. But discipleship without a cost is not discipleship. The price of discipleship is high, but the cost of our non-discipleship is much higher for those without Christ.

Some prospective disciples of Christ disqualified themselves by considering the cost and counting it too high. Jesus told one would-be follower to sell all his possessions and come and follow Him, but he walked away after considering the cost. The words He spoke recorded in Luke 14:26 make me cringe: "If anyone comes to Me and does not hate his father and mother, wife and children, brothers and sisters, yes, and his own life also, he cannot be My disciple." This is intense to say the least! Was Jesus requiring His followers to hate their parents and siblings? Jesus addressed some of the most important relationships a human can have, but He was sending a message: Following Him is not for the onlookers, the causal, or the fans. Following Him is for the sold out, the committed, and the hard core, even if you are disowned by your family.

What did Jesus mean in Luke 9:23 when He required His disciples to deny themselves and to take up their cross and follow Him? This may be one of the most misunderstood commands of Jesus. The word *deny* means to "resist," "reject," or "refuse." To deny yourself does not mean to deny your appearance, DNA, pedigree, career, emotions, or intelligence. Denying yourself simply means to dethrone yourself as lord of your own life. It means to deny yourself of your right to live selfishly with no consideration of a purpose other than your own. Before we can pray "thy kingdom come," we must first be willing to pray "my kingdom go." Perhaps the power of the idea of denying ourselves has been diminished by a misunderstanding of what it means to take up our cross.

Anyone who has been around the church awhile has heard various people bemoan their maladies, hardships, and personal difficulties only to resign themselves to these troubling issues as their cross to bear. But Jesus meant much more than this. This interpretation falls short of what Jesus was requiring of His followers. The believer's personal cross of Christianity does not refer to the challenges and sacrifices that hardships of life introduce to us, nor does it refer to bearing the things that we have given up to walk with the Lord. No believer has given up anything to walk with Christ and spend eternity with Him that they wouldn't have had to give up anyway to be eternally lost.

Anyone carrying a cross in first-century Judea knew that the day was not going to end well. A criminal who was carrying his own cross knew he was a dead man (or at least he would be within a few hours) and had abandoned all earthly hopes and ambitions. In this command, Jesus was calling His disciples to think of themselves as dead to this world along with all their worldly hopes, ambitions, and dreams, and allow the plans, hopes, and dreams of Jesus Christ to arise within them.

What did Jesus mean in Matthew 16:25 when He said, "For whoever desires to save his life will lose it, but whoever loses his life for My sake will find it"? It's simple: When we find our lives in the context of this world and do not follow Christ, we will ultimately lose everything. We may find great success by the world's standards, but when our lives are over we will lose absolutely everything by leaving it all behind. However, when we lose that life and give it up for Christ's sake by investing all we are and have for His gospel's sake, we will find our purpose and abundant life in Christ. How could we lose our life any more than when we deny ourselves of our own agenda, calendar, and resources, and begin investing it all in our disciples?

So how do we know if we qualify to be a disciple of Jesus Christ today? I think this question can be answered by asking: Who is your disciple? Believers whose lives are invested daily in the lives of sinners and friends in an attempt to make disciples out of them qualify as disciples of Jesus Christ. Those who are daily living out their lives intentionally with others in mind, and are building relationships with lost people, and have denied themselves, taken up their cross, and demonstrated that they are willing to forsake all to follow in His footsteps, have achieved the biblical distinction of twenty-first-century disciples of Jesus Christ. Pastors, let's go make disciples who make disciples.

Questions for discussion:

* What would be your definition of a disciple in the first century and how would that compare to being a disciple today?

* Why do you think Jesus spoke differently to uncommitted people than He did to His disciples?

* How does the picture of carrying a cross speak to the commitment of making a disciple?

CHAPTER 7

THE GREAT COMMISSION:
CHURCH DEPARTMENT
OR CHURCH CULTURE?

Every local church must decide if it is going to fulfill the Great Commission and engage every believer in disciple making or merely assign that job to a department. Some congregations have well-operating ministries with one designated as "evangelism" or "outreach." If a local church has people leading a ministry who spend most of their time thinking about how the church is going to make an impact in their community, then they are further down the road in fulfilling the Great Commission than most. It is good to have such a ministry in the church. However, designating only one ministry to fulfill the purpose of the church will probably limit the number of people working in that area. Those who are not directly involved in that ministry may feel they are already doing their own ministry and don't need to be involved in making disciples.

Some churches may endeavor to make disciples on the side but Jesus commanded His church to be a disciple-making church. It has been said a jack of all trades is a master of none. Churches that try to do everything will be proficient in nothing, but churches that focus on one thing will be successful. Paul was a successful leader, author, church planter, and disciple maker because he streamlined his daily agenda. He did not say, "These many things I tinker around with" but he said, "This one thing I do" (Philippians 3:13). As long as making disciples falls under just one program in the church there will never be a culture of disciple making within the heart and soul of the church. How much more powerful it would be to have disciple making at the center of every ministry, and on the mind, heart, and lips of the pastor(s), staff, teams, and members of the congregation.

Solomon was absolutely correct when he said, "Where there is no vision, the people perish" (Proverbs 29:18, KJV). A vision is a compelling picture of the future that inspires passion. A river has banks that provide definition, purpose, and flow. The restraint of the riverbanks harnesses the power of the river, which can provide momentum for travel and energy. Without the restraint of the banks, the river would become a swamp. Without the discipline of vision, a local church can become a magnet for every idea and brainstorm imaginable. Without a vision, a local church will be powerless to say no to every impulse that comes floating by. By possessing a vision, the power and energy within a local church can become an unstoppable force.

Through the years I have observed ministries and churches that have become distracted from the mission. I know of one pastor who taught and preached about the oneness of God in every church service for eight years. Now don't get me wrong, the oneness of God is the greatest revelation of Scripture and I love to hear it taught, but this is out of balance. It's easy to preach about what you're for or what you're against, but this doesn't fulfill the mission of the church. Pastors are called to cast a vision, create a path to get there, and then lead the people faithfully until the vision comes to pass.

What gets preached or rewarded will get done in a local church. I read about a church in a small community that offered a chicken dinner with all the fixings as a weekend fundraiser. They had some excellent cooks in the church so, predictably, the fundraiser went well. Not only did they raise a lot of money but folks in the community enjoyed the food and began asking for another dinner. The next month they supplied the demand and did it all over again. Well, these chicken dinners became all the rage in this small community so the pastor decided that they would begin offering dinners every weekend. Business was booming and word on the street accelerated until the workload demanded that everyone in the church become involved. Sunday school teachers helped, ushers and greeters rolled up their shirtsleeves, choir members started helping, and the young people began making deliveries on their bicycles. Profits were healthy, church people were excited, and the community was happy and demanded more.

The pastor decided that instead of midweek service they would dedicate that time to sell dinners to the community; after all, it was ministry. It wasn't long until they also gave up their Sunday night service to prepare for the dinner demands of the coming week. You can see where this is going. Eventually they just stopped having church and turned their facility into a take-out chicken dinner restaurant. Maybe you've heard of it: Churches Chicken. Well, the punch line is not true

(I couldn't resist), but the rest of the story actually happened. What if that church would have had the same organization, passion, and energy for making disciples? Every church will have a culture for sure, but how exciting it is when the culture is about daily reaching lost people. Elder T. F. Tenney used to say, "The main thing is to keep the main thing the main thing."

Years ago, not much was said about culture within the context of an organization. A culture was something observed in a Petri dish or in a lab through a microscope, but in recent years, the term has become widespread. Organizational culture is especially important when there are teams involved. It is easy but counterproductive for teams within an organization to do their own thing and not communicate, cooperate, or complement each other. But when the culture in a church organization is about making disciples, then every team, ministry, and department must be on the same page and partner together to accomplish the shared goal.

While it is true that vision will set your direction, it is also true that it is the culture that will take you there. You can have the most amazing vision that captures the imagination of your congregation, but without the appropriate culture the vision will never materialize. If you have a healthy church culture but no vision, you may have a good time, but you will never move forward. Possessing culture with no vision is like the pilot who came over the intercom and announced to the passengers that he had some bad news and some good news. He said, "The bad news is that we have lost all use of our flying instruments and we don't have a clue where we are or where we're going. But the good news is that we have picked up a tailwind and are making record time."

Vision can be cast in a day but culture occurs daily. Very little disciple making occurs on Sunday. In fact, effective disciple making must go beyond a class that meets once a week on Sunday morning. Disciples must be made one at a time, or at the most, a few at a time. This kind of disciple making does not happen just on Sundays, but must also happen Monday through Saturday. This is culture.

Vision is a compelling picture of the future, but a vision cannot be demonstrated until culture makes it a reality. Too many great messages have been preached and visions have been cast to reach the world with little or nothing to show for it. The saints hear these messages and get up from the altar more determined than ever to reach the world, but nothing ever changes. They remain barren and feel guilty for not making a difference, but there is no church culture of disciple making to feed and equip their weekly pursuit of lost people.

It appears from the scriptural narrative that Jesus intended for His disciples of all succeeding generations to go make disciples until He returns. One would be hard-pressed to read the Book of Acts and the New Testament epistles and arrive at any other conclusion. In fact, any believer claiming to be a Christian and an ardent follower of Jesus Christ can find no wiggle room in this area of Christian living and personal discipline. Every born-again believer is qualified and capable of taking someone on the journey of becoming a disciple.

One of the most important leadership axioms regarding the subject of making disciples is that people do not do what we say, but do what we do. The most powerful demonstration a pastor or leader can give concerning reaching the world with the gospel is to model disciple making. This modeling must go beyond preaching convicting sermons about reaching the lost, leading staff members, raising children, welcoming guests, writing visitor follow-up letters, making phone calls to recent guests, and all of the other necessary administrative things for a church to function. The single greatest action a pastor can take to influence the congregation is to personally model disciple making.

This is an area where a lab-coat-technician approach will not work. A leader who doesn't model disciple making will not successfully inspire or motivate others to be disciple makers. In my opinion, no leader that is called into the fivefold ministry is exempt from the command to go make disciples. The first-century apostles certainly did not exempt themselves from making disciples. Paul always had young men traveling with him as he developed them on the go. He knew the impact that Barnabas's nurturing had upon his personal life and early ministry, and therefore continued this model throughout his life. Peter brought Mark under his purview and oversaw his personal growth (I Peter 5:13).

Believers who are involved in full-time ministry with a local church are not exempt from the call to go make disciples, despite the fact that they may be doing the "Lord's work" all day long. Their job description may include making phone calls, sending letters, and other administrative responsibilities, but their calling is to make disciples. Employees in a local church are not excused from making disciples, whether they are working in daycare, the Christian school, administration, or custodial services. There is no substitute activity for your hands-on involvement with a spiritually lost individual that God has placed in your life, and to lead that person gently to the Word, the gospel, the altar, the baptismal water, and into a brand new life in Christ.

Jesus demonstrated the behavior He wanted to see reproduced in His followers. His model of leadership was not one of pontificating from a high horse and requiring His subjects to engage in all sorts of behavior that He had no intention of performing Himself. Leaders who do this are dangerous to themselves and to the organization they lead. This type of leadership style can lead to corruption and failure. Instead, Jesus exemplified every action, attitude, and behavior He desired to see reproduced in His followers. He said, "He who believes in Me, the works that I do he will do also" (John 14:12).

It has been said that we teach what we know but we reproduce what we are. Jesus was the greatest teacher human ears have ever heard, but He was also the greatest servant-leader that the world has ever seen. It is no wonder that His disciples were willing to take a nail for Him when they saw Him do it for them. He reproduced His qualities of selfless love and compassion in them. Jesus was not an ivory tower kind of leader, but rather, He was approachable, reachable, and touchable. He was up close and personal with the Twelve and was continually with them, training, teaching, demonstrating, and then observing them do ministry. His method of disciple making was that He did it and they watched, then they did it and He watched, and then they did it (Acts 1:1; Luke 10:1–21). He expected His followers to be disciples who made disciples. He modeled it, taught it, inspected it, and gave them a picture of doing it after He was gone.

Churches that have leaders who model disciple making will undoubtedly begin to see the same practice reproduced in the members of the congregation. Every Sunday our goal is to have a disciple-making testimony. There are few things more exciting than hearing the stories of changed lives both by the disciples and their makers. It's even more exciting when testimonies are shared by second and third generation disciples. This is when the church begins to move from addition to multiplication.

Every pastor knows the joy and pain of casting a vision. Pastors also know the thrill of hearing everyone talk about the vision, but also the frustration when they are the only ones talking about the vision. You know a vision is beginning to get traction when staff members begin to synthesize it among themselves. When they initiate conversations, text messages, and emails with the pastor and other members of the congregation, then something good is going to happen. It's exciting when members of the congregation begin using the buzz words and phrases introduced by the pastor during vision casting. When that begins to happen, then you know you've got boots on the ground. When the church knows that its mission is to make disciples, when there are more prayer requests about their disciples than their personal problems, when their testimonies are more about changed lives and less about overcoming their challenges, when their prayers are more focused on others, then you know that the culture has changed.

Is it unrealistic to expect that every mature believer in a local congregation could become a disciple maker? Maybe, but why not take this vision as far as you can? Some have said that a local church only needs one soulwinner to make it grow. There is no doubt this is true, especially if that person is especially gifted and anointed. But it was not Jesus' plan that only one person in every congregation would be gifted in getting people to the altar and to the water, and then pray them through. This model tends to create superhero soulwinners. Such a model gives a congregation a false sense that only a select few are gifted to reach the world, and there is nothing more the average saint needs to do.

Our local church has just such a gifted full-time staff member. He is used greatly by God with an incomparable heart for lost people. He never meets a stranger, and through the Word can get people to the water with great success. He recently told me that he had no problem teaching Bible studies but did not know what to do with people when the study was completed. He could continue to spend all of his time teaching Bible studies, and we would continue to see many baptisms through his efforts alone, but over the last few years he has been training others how to teach Bible studies, bring sinners to conversion, and lead them to spiritual maturity.

Thank God that many congregations have people in them with this passion and skill set. But I believe it is possible to create a culture within a local church where the spiritual DNA of disciple making becomes embedded in every fiber of its existence. Making disciples should not merely be a program situated under a departmental heading where only one or a few are engaged. Every believer may not be willing, but every believer is capable of making a disciple. Making disciples must become the focus of every ministry from children to seniors. Men's, ladies, young adult, youth, and children's ministries should have a disciple-making purpose in everything they do.

Every pastor has a dream. I have a dream that all members of the congregation will rise up and fulfill the Great Commission in their personal lives. I dream that we will not try to fulfill this commission through institutionalized programs or artificially created events but that we will daily live intentionally with a disciple-maker's vision and heart. I dream that our members will not just faithfully give their missions offerings and feel as though they have relieved themselves of the burden to go make disciples of all nations. I dream that the congregation will not believe that it is the pastor's job and that of the full-time staff and one or two triple-A personality types to make disciples in the community.

I dream that one day every born-again believer will realize and accept the Christ-given mission to go make disciples. I dream that everyone in our congregation will walk into every room with an attitude of "There you are" instead of "Here I am." I dream that every mature believer will turn sinners into friends and friends into disciples, and that they will not just follow but follow to lead others. I have a dream that every born-again Apostolic Christian will continually have a disciple at his or her side. What would happen in our communities, our cities, our nation, and the world if this was the dream of every pastor and the culture of every local Apostolic church?

Questions for discussion:

- What is the difference between a program-based church and a relationship-building church?

- What is the difference between having an outreach department in a church and being a disciple-making church?

- How can a church go from presenting a vision to cultivating a culture?

CHAPTER 8

WHO IS MY NEIGHBOR?
THE GREATEST QUESTION
FOR A TROUBLED WORLD

"Who is my neighbor?" Jesus was asked this question in Luke 10. Rather than give a direct answer, Jesus told a compelling story that I would invite you to consider within a disciple-making context.

"Who is my neighbor?" may be the most important question of this hour. The future harmony of humanity rests in the answer to this question. We live in an unprecedented age of worldwide crisis including terrorism, hatred, murder, racism, bigotry, atrocities perpetrated against children, divorce, religious genocide (just to name a few). The good news is that there is an answer. Obedience to the gospel of Jesus Christ will cure every social ill, and at no cost to the taxpayers. Unfortunately, no politician would run a campaign suggesting that obedience to the gospel and becoming a disciple of Jesus Christ would all but end teen pregnancy, abortion, STDs, addiction, domestic violence, and other such problems.

In 2015 Lee Stoneking was invited to address the United Nations along with thirteen other speakers.

Their given subject was to present solutions to end world violence. None of the other speakers had answers, but Brother Stoneking shared his testimony of being miraculously raised from the dead, followed by a simple presentation of the gospel encapsulated in Acts 2:38. His concluding remark was, "Ladies and gentlemen, I give you Jesus." When we give Jesus to another human being, we are answering the question, "Who is my neighbor?"

The thoughtful answer to the question, "Who is my neighbor?" could ostensibly end all war, murder, hatred, gossip, crime, rioting, and violent protests. The answer of "I give you Jesus" could not only begin to provide an answer for some deplorable world conditions, but also fulfill the mission of Christ. The Lord's ground forces, called disciples, offer the change that would make disciples of all nations and potentially eradicate all of these issues and ills from the face of the earth.

In my view, the church is lacking a compelling sense of responsibility to those around us. We cannot be responsible for others but we must be responsible to others. I mean this in the sense of social justice as well as having a heart for the eternal destinies of lost people. Our Western culture projects an independent spirit and objects to any accountability that imposes restrictions on our freedoms. Jesus warned us that the spirit of offense would rise in the last days. Truly we are seeing that prophecy fulfilled through things such as political correctness and frivolous lawsuits that dominate national and social media. This world would benefit from a return to the old-fashioned "neighborly" spirit; a kinder, gentler, more tolerant disposition toward people who are not just like us.

Paul demonstrated our responsibility to others when he wrote, "I had no rest in my spirit, because I did not find Titus my brother" (II Corinthians 2:13). Paul looked around and noticed someone was missing. Whose job is it to notice when someone is missing in your house, your office, your classroom, and most importantly, in your local church? Is it the pastor's job? Is it the hospitality ministry's job? Yes, it is their job and calling, but it is also our individual responsibility.

One of the saddest and often repeated tragedies is for someone to die at home but remain undiscovered for several days because nobody missed that person. If your neighbor is missing from your local church (you know who they are; we all sit in our same seats every Sunday) then it's your job to notice and to check on that person. Just pick up your phone, contact that person, and express your concern. The heart of a disciple maker is to notice who is not there. Don't pass off that responsibility to someone else. You can start making disciples right in the neighborhood of your own worship center. May your spirit find no rest until you locate your missing neighbor.

The heart of a disciple maker is not altogether different than that of a parent. Parents never stop worrying about their children, even after they become responsible adults. And when the grandchildren come along, they are added to the worry list. Parents never rest until they locate their children in a store, at the park, in the backyard, or in the sanctuary. When they eyeball their loved one, then all is well in the world. Why could we not have the same restlessness in our spirit for absent saints, lost neighbors, or for new believers who have missed a few church services? They are our neighbors.

Luke 15 is the lost and found chapter. How long did it take the father to notice one of two sons was gone? How long did it take the shepherd to notice one of the one hundred sheep was missing? How long did it take the woman to notice one coin from her dowry was out of place? In each case they were proactive in searching for them. The father diligently watched and waited until he saw his prodigal son afar off. The woman who lost her coin got out a broom and thoroughly swept the house until she found it. The shepherd didn't have the attitude that ninety-nine were enough, but would not rest until he searched and found his lost sheep. Look around; who's missing?

Jesus was asked the question, "Who is my neighbor?" in Luke 10:29. The doctor of the Law who asked Jesus this question first asked him what he must do to merit eternal life. Jesus responded by asking him what the Law said about it. He correctly responded in verse 27, "You shall love the LORD your God with all your heart, with all your soul, with all your strength, and with all your mind, and your neighbor as yourself." It appears that the procurement of eternal life is connected to our love for God and loving our neighbor. We can understand why loving God is part of the answer to the eternal life question, but why does loving our neighbor have anything to do with eternity?

One piece of the answer to this question should be obvious: If we love God with all our heart, soul, strength, and mind, then it should follow that we will love the things that God loves, and God loves the lost (John 3:16). In fact, if we honor the first commandment and keep it active and flowing in our lives, we would not need to be reminded of the other nine commandments. For example, if we love God as prescribed by Scripture, then we will not have any other gods before us, and we will not lie, steal, covet, commit adultery, or murder. If we love God this way and allow His love to flow through us, then we naturally will love our neighbor as ourselves.

The golden rule teaches us to treat others the way we would like to be treated. I'm not sure how anyone can inherit eternal life by only loving God and themselves. The kingdom of God doesn't work that way. Jesus said, "But if you do not forgive men their trespasses, neither will your Father forgive your trespasses" (Matthew 6:15). He indexed our receiving forgiveness from God to our willingness (or unwilling-ness) to forgive others. The questions remain however; "Who is your neighbor?" and "How do you love your neighbor as yourself?"

The entirety of Luke 10 is specifically focused on the mission of Jesus Christ and the church. Early in the chapter Jesus sent out seventy of His disciples to do ministry. When they returned with their joyful reports of victory, Jesus rejoiced with them. How exciting this must have been for both this Rabbi and His disciples. This was the first trial run by Jesus' disciples, which was a precursor to how the Kingdom would work after Jesus returned to Heaven and had sent the Holy Spirit. The Rabbi was rewarded to see that His power and principles were being exercised by His disciples with good results. The disciples were excited to learn that what they had been taught by their Rabbi really worked.

I would suggest that the theme in Luke 10 did not change when the doctor of the Law asked Jesus who his neighbor was. I would further suggest that Jesus did not change the subject and shift to some other idea when answering his question. It appears to me that, contextually, the work of the seventy earlier in the chapter is tied to the "neighbor" question toward the end of the chapter. In the parable of the Good Samaritan, Jesus was not merely presenting an image of being socially responsible to those in our path who have been beaten by the hardships of life. He was clearly demonstrating the heart, obligation, and responsibility of a disciple maker.

Any individual believer or a congregation that desires to make disciples of necessity must embrace an "everyone is welcome" mentality and attitude. The story that Jesus told in response to the question, "Who is my neighbor?" shook up the religious mindset of that era. As you probably know, the Jews ran a closed shop. They viewed Gentiles as "dogs" and the Samaritans (mixed ancestry between Jews and Gentiles) as something even less. The Jews traversing from Galilee to Judea would take a detour and cross the Jordan River twice so as not to have to set foot in Samaria. This is why it was notable to the disciples when Jesus said that He needed to go through Samaria (John 4:4). This dynamic is the backdrop for when Jesus explained to them who their neighbor was.

It is instructive to observe how Jesus positioned the characters in this story. You might have predicted He would have situated a Jewish person as the one in a position to welcome an "outsider" but instead He set the Samaritan in this role. I would imagine Christ did this to make an even greater impact with His illustration. Jews would not lift a finger to assist a Samaritan and certainly would not expect any overtures from a Samaritan toward a Jew in need. When Jesus assigned the Samaritan as the one in a position to help the Jewish man, this further implicated their guilt in failing to obey the two greatest commandments and to treat all other humans with love, kindness, and respect.

In the ancient Near East, hospitality was extended to whoever needed it, strangers and acquaintances alike. In fact, in its original form, the word *hospitality* was derived from two separate words; one word meaning "friend" and the other meaning "stranger." So, from the beginning of its usage, hospitality included the idea of making friends out of strangers. One significant message from the parable of the Good Samaritan is that our neighbor may well be a complete stranger in every sense of the word.

Disciple makers not only have an "others first" attitude but they are not exclusive when it comes to who those others are. True disciples of Christ don't just see strangers for who or what they appear to be outwardly; they look beneath the surface and see strangers as potential neighbors in the body of Christ. We have all seen people who startle us with their appearance, such as elaborate tattoos, multiple piercings, unusually colored hair, and so on, but underneath we know there is a hurting, broken heart that needs Jesus.

I'm so thankful for my daughter Micaela, who possesses a disciple maker's heart. She has developed friendships among some girls she attends college with who are of the Islamic faith. She and my wife have been in one of their homes to observe their study of the Quran. They were treated with fine hospitality. We are excited to be hosting several of these young ladies in our home in just a few days from this writing. (With a rapid rise of violence perpetrated by radical Muslims in this world, the only answer to this problem is the gospel of Jesus Christ.) Her neighbors are not like her and your neighbor is not like you.

Jesus was accused by His detractors of being the friend of publicans and sinners (Matthew 11:19). Is there evidence in our lives that we could be accused of the same? Jesus' method of making disciples was to engage sinners (strangers) and turn them into friends. Many of His friends eventually became His disciples. It should be noted, however, that Jesus did not choose disciples who were just like Him. He was a carpenter from an inland town named Nazareth. Most of His disciples were fishermen from communities located near the Sea of Galilee. Yet despite their differences, He befriended them, invested in them, and made loyal disciples out of them.

If we could call the sanctuary where you worship a "neighborhood," who would you allow to become your neighbor? Who would you permit to move in and live right beside you in your neighborhood (pew)? Local congregations must decide who is welcome in their neighborhoods (sanctuaries). Who are you willing to worship with? Who are you willing to pray with? Who are you willing to share your life with? Who are you willing to put your arm around or whose head are you willing to lay your hand on in prayer?

I told our congregation one day that my favorite smell in church is cigarette smoke. I noticed frowns on some sanctified faces. Then I said, "My second favorite smell in church is alcohol" (more disgusted looks). It got worse: "My third favorite smell in church is body odor" (some were about ready to get sick and leave). It should be obvious to disciple makers why I would make statements like this. If those aromas are in the "neighborhood" then that means somebody needs Jesus. Isaac said to Jacob, "The smell of my son is as the smell of the field that the Lord has blessed" (Genesis 27:27). We need to welcome the smell of the field into our congregations. Neighbors smell unclean when they are entertaining unclean spirits. The Holy Spirit will convict them, and their obedience to the gospel will clean up their lives as we make disciples out of them.

When guests walk into your worship space, they are looking for three things: (1) unconditional love, (2) unconditional acceptance, and (3) to picture themselves as belonging. The greatest human need is the desire to belong. Visitors to your church want to be able to imagine themselves as part of your congregation. Therefore, it's important that they see themselves on the platform and in the congregation.

I have discovered that not every congregation is ready or willing to embrace a Luke 10:29 neighbor. They may be singing "Rescue the Perishing" but they may be living "Hold the Fort." I served a small congregation that had not baptized anyone in two years before we came alongside them. The baptistery was dry and had become a spiderweb condominium. God blessed us and gave us sixteen baptisms within our first three months. We naturally thought everyone would be excited about new neighbors in the neighborhood. After all, reaching lost people is not exactly a novel idea for an Apostolic church. Corporate America loves new customers, but not this group.

We were shocked at the negative response of possibly the greatest revival they had ever seen in their history. Many outrageous comments and gestures were made in reaction to the new neighbors. Some complained about snotty-nosed kids rubbing their dirty hands on their freshly painted walls. Others discredited any move toward God that they did not personally observe and sanctimoniously endorse. They accused our new disciples of being charismatic because they did not see them repent at an old-fashioned altar. I was quick to inform them that they had already repented with tears at their kitchen tables and living room couches long before they ever came to church.

I'm not exactly sure how these people would have interpreted the purpose of Jesus' parable about the Good Samaritan. In their minds it may have meant stopping to help someone change a flat tire or assist an elderly person crossing the street. Their "Boy Scout religion" mentality probably included keeping their grass cut, picking up newspapers in the driveway, paying their bills on time, and not annoying anyone (as if that would reach the world). To be sure, something could be said for these attributes, and without them our testimony would be hindered, but Jesus had much more in mind than this when He answered the question, "Who is my neighbor?"

One day I went to the house of a family I was discipling in that town. The wife and young children had visited the church a few times, but the husband was an alcoholic and did not participate in the Bible studies we had around the kitchen table. Instead, he watched TV in the living room. When I knocked on the door, their four-year-old son opened the door. When he saw me his eyes got big and he turned around and yelled, "Hey Mom, God's here!" The husband was not a good man. The ravages of alcohol had taken a toll on him and the family. He called me one day from a detox center and said he was ready to repent. I let him dry out for a few more days and then went to visit him. We agonized in prayer together for over an hour as he wept his way to repentance. He was soon baptized and filled with the Holy Spirit. We made disciples of them and I'm thankful to report they are pillars (and not strangers) in that congregation yet today.

Latent within the parable of the Good Samaritan is the inescapable idea that your neighbor is not like you. Our typical default when it comes to choosing neighbors is that we generally gravitate toward people like us. All of the adages apply: kind begets kind, birds of a feather flock together, water seeks its own level, you can't attract what you want but what you are, and so forth. However, when Jesus identified his neighbor to the lawyer who asked the question, I'm sure he was surprised to learn that according to Jesus' standards, his neighbor was nothing like him. The primary difference, from which all other disparities trickled down, was that one was a Jew, and the other was a Samaritan.

Another important aspect of this account is that Jesus positioned the Jew in the story as the man who was beaten, dying, and in need of help. The Samaritan was the neighbor who was well, able-bodied, and situated to be able to provide care. For a Jewish man to be in such a predicament as to having been ignored by his Jewish religious community, and then needing the intervention of any available human being, especially a Samaritan, was embarrassing and humiliating. Jesus could have switched the roles, making the Samaritan the one in need, but He emphasized the attitude of a Christlike neighbor by positioning the characters as He did.

I think the message for us here is that it is not always obvious or natural to connect with the neighbors that God places in our path. The priest and the Levite walked right by their fellow Jewish neighbor. The Good Samaritan was on his way to some far-away destination, but this wayside opportunity gripped his heart, changed his itinerary, and engaged his hands. Sensitive disciple makers go through their daily routines watching, listening, and stopping long enough to see if there is some cry or crisis that they can serve.

If our disciple maker's lens allows us only to perceive the needs of people like us, then we may miss the point of this critical narrative. The old adage, opposites attract, is not any truer than in the story Jesus told.

The behavior of the Good Samaritan was similar to the initial behavior that a disciple maker must have when engaging a potential disciple. He walked across the street (leaving his side of the street) and came to the opposite side of the road where his neighbor was. He assessed his new neighbor's condition (in-take triage) and immediately knew what to do. He made a commitment right then to encumber himself with the trouble of another human being, going out of his way to pour oil and wine out of his own resources. He bandaged his wounds, lifted him up on his own beast, and took him to a safe place of recovery. But he didn't stop there. He paid the innkeeper out of his own pocket and said he would make a follow-up visit to see what else needed to be done to get this man back on his feet. All of these actions perfectly describe the attitude, assessment, and actions necessary to be a disciple maker.

Every mature believer must ask himself or herself the question that the Good Samaritan asked: "Is this my neighbor?" When we answer this question correctly, a chain of events will begin to unfold. We must get on the same side of the street as our neighbor or by definition we don't have a neighbor. When you begin traveling with a neighbor, expect to slow down and not arrive as fast as you could if you were traveling alone. Your journey will now take more time, cost more money, and involve more responsibility. Your Christlike spirit of love, forgiveness, and acceptance will be the oil and wine to your disciple's spirit. Others in life have beaten them but your love will restore them. Ultimately, the time you spend with them will be a safe place of recovery and healing.

I have lived in eight different neighborhoods in my lifetime. I know people who have moved dozens of times. When we choose a neighborhood to buy a home in, we typically research good property values, investigate the home association that upholds those property values, check out the schools, notice how convenient the shopping is, and of course, check out the neighbors. Once all the dynamics are suited to our liking, we make the purchase and move in.

When you choose a neighborhood, you choose your neighbors. But once you move in, you cannot choose your neighbors anymore. Your future neighbors will choose you. In much the same respect, when we choose a local church, we inspect and check out everything: location, attitude, doctrine, pastor, leadership, opportunities, culture. When we find a church that merits our approval, we move in. But once we choose a church, we no longer have a say about who the new neighbors are going to be.

I like thinking of a lost people as "my neighbors." Somehow calling them "neighbors" removes some of the fear and anxiety that typically accompanies the pursuit of a new relationship. Maybe Mr. Rogers had it right in his old children's program for PBS. He unconditionally welcomed all children into his neighborhood. He offered acceptance and celebrated every child for who they were. He often said, "Did you know there's not anyone in the world exactly like you? And there was no one like you before you, and there will never be another one like you after. I like you just the way you are." Mr. Rogers' kind manner and soft voice disarmed children and made them feel comfortable while watching his program. Let's not miss his powerful message of acceptance. Of course we love the lost for who they are, but we know that God loves them too much to leave them the way He found them.

The end-time revival is clearly a multicultural revival much like it was at the beginning. Joel prophesied that the Holy Spirit would be poured out upon all flesh. On the Day of Pentecost devout Jews gathered in Jerusalem from every nation under Heaven (Acts 2:5). We understand this to be hyperbolic language, but nevertheless there were seventeen groups and nationalities specifically mentioned. Of course it didn't take long afterward for the Holy Spirit to fall on the other two biblical categories of people, the Samaritans and the Gentiles (Acts 8; 10). Pastors, church leaders, and members must lovingly welcome neighbors who may not look anything like them.

In chapter 3 I mentioned one of my current disciples, my literal neighbor, who lives across the street from me. My wife and I walked across the street two years ago with a plate of homemade chocolate chip cookies to introduce ourselves to him. This was the same day that the SWAT team came to his house and arrested his wife. They had only been our neighbors for a few weeks and we had not actually met them yet. He was clearly shaken up when he met us at the door. Nothing came of the seed planted that day until two years later. On Labor Day we were pulling into our driveway after returning from a trip and he came running over to our house. He was asking some pretty heavy questions. Since that day I have been in his house nearly every week, spending at least two hours per visit talking about life, God, and His Word.

My neighbor and I have little in common. He is black and I am white. He was raised in a dysfunctional home whereas mine was more balanced. He grew up in a poor neighborhood and I in a middle class neighborhood. His home and neighborhood was filled with violence but this is a life I know nothing about. His mother shot and killed his brother right before his eyes. She is in prison today. My mother was an angel and is in Paradise. He struggles with forgiving his mother, something I cannot identify with.

He is retired from a successful military career. I never served in the military. He has been through two marriages and I have been married for thirty-eight years. But despite all of the differences and lack of common ground, he is my literal and biblical neighbor and I love his precious life and that of his two dear children. We have become good friends and occasionally go to lunch together and chat on the sidewalk. I have attended a few of his nine-year-old son's basketball games. At the time of this writing, I have yet to invite him to come to church because I know that one day he will invite himself. He is my neighbor. Who is your neighbor?

The local church should reflect the community in which it serves. If a local church is in a multicultural community or city but their membership consists of only one nationality, then they are not reaching the whole community. The militant church on earth should reflect the triumphant church in Heaven. John saw that church in Revelation 5:9, "And they sang a new song, saying: 'You are worthy to take the scroll, and to open its seals; for you were slain, and have redeemed us to God by your blood out of every tribe and tongue and people and nation.'"

According to this verse, it appears that by the time of the coming of the Lord, the church will have fulfilled the mission given to us by the Founder to go make disciples of all nations. Does your congregation reflect the demographics of your community? If so, then it is obvious you have discovered the answer to the question, "Who is my neighbor?" If not, let there be no rest in your spirit until you discover your neighbor who may not be like you.

I cannot close this chapter without asking you, the reader, "Who is your neighbor?" And more specifically, "Who is your disciple?" Can you identify a lost person or a brand new believer that you personally feel responsible for? Will you come alongside that believer in his or her spiritual transformation? If not, maybe you should take another look at Hebrews 5:12 (NLT): "You have been believers so long now that you ought to be teaching others. Instead, you need someone to teach you again the basic things about God's word."

How long does a Christian need to believe before he graduates from milk to meat? How long does she need to be saved before she is teaching others? I know people who have been saved and sanctified in the church for years and yet somehow do not feel qualified to make disciples. This is not the plan of God for our lives. The writer of Hebrews apparently was aware of good saints of God who were doing nothing to make disciples. He clearly stated that failing to make disciples is the profile of an immature believer. He then stated that making disciples (i.e., teaching others) is one of the most basic things about God's Word. Making disciples is not God's PhD program, but an elementary school level of understanding and behavior. The vast majority of mature Apostolic Christians are over-qualified to make a disciple.

Too many mature Christians are educated way beyond their level of obedience. Isn't it time to raise our level of obedience to our level of biblical education? Let us obey the Great Commission and go and make disciples, and let's begin with our neighbor.

Questions for discussion:

* How could the answer to the question, "Who is my neighbor?" potentially change the world?

* How do we gain influence with people from other cultures?

* What fears do you need to overcome before connecting with someone who is not like you?

CHAPTER 9

DISCIPLE MAKERS AS TOUR GUIDES:

EVERYONE NEEDS NAVIGATION

If you have ever been on a tour to a strange city or nation, then you may understand how wonderful it is to have a local guide. I have been on several tours to the Holy Land with various tour guides. I can testify that the quality of tour guide makes all the difference. The sites are all the same, the buses, food, and hotels are all similar. But the tour guide determines the level of enrichment in your experience. Nearly everything you see, hear, and feel as you take the journey is directly downloaded to you after having been filtered through the background, education, experience, and attitude of your guide. A good guide is worth his or her weight in Solomon's gold.

Jesus commanded all of His disciples in every generation to go and make disciples (Matthew 28:19). He did not speak these words analogously or meta-phorically, but His directive should be literally taken to heart by every serious Christian. As we have discussed throughout this book, a disciple is one who follows to lead. Jesus said if the blind lead the blind they both fall into the ditch. A disciple maker is like a tour guide who leads the new believer into a new and undiscovered life.

The whole disciple-making motif of developing mature Christians is somewhat of a vague illustration to Western minds. Not until recent years has mentoring become in vogue for job orientation in corporate America. However, disciple making was an integral part of first-century Jewish culture. Jesus did not give His future followers the prerogative of determining what would be the best or most effective way to establish spiritual maturity in new believers of a given culture. Jesus' disciple-making model was intended for disciples of every generation and century to replicate continuously.

In the rabbi-disciple dynamic of the first century, the rabbi typically invited a prospective disciple into a mentoring relationship. This required a commitment both on the part of the rabbi and the student. In this relationship, the rabbi would lead and the disciple followed. The rabbi interpreted Scripture, shared his ideas and philosophies about God and Torah, and intentionally shared his knowledge and wisdom concerning life situations with his young protégés.

It is obviously true that disciple makers must be more mature in their walk with God than their followers or there will be no transformation. A disciple maker must be someone worth following. It is not necessary for someone who desires to make disciples to achieve ultimate Christian perfection before he or she attempts to make disciples. In fact, if this were the requirement, none of us would qualify.

The most important thing about a leader-follower relationship is that the leader must be more mature in Christ than the follower. Leaders lead by staying ahead, but not too far ahead. In fact, it is actually only necessary for the mentor to be one step ahead. We encourage our new believers to immediately begin to share their faith and testimony with their friends even before they completely obey the gospel. For example, if they have successfully repented, then they can begin to mentor their friends in repentance and so on.

Disciple makers understand that if they want the message and mission of Christ to carry on after they are gone, they must replace themselves. Too many mature believers live their daily lives like they will live forever. They fail to invest everything that they've become personally and intentionally into someone who will outlive them. The tragic result is that their spirit, heart, walk with Christ, and knowledge of God will go with them to the grave.

Moses was a great leader but he did not take all of his leadership abilities, gifts, and knowledge to the grave. He invested time and energy in the next generation leader named Joshua. He invited Joshua to closely follow him. He took Joshua to places and shared experiences that no other Israelite was given the opportunity to capture. When he was informed by God that he would not be taking the Israelites into the Promised Land, the "hand-off" to Joshua became even more urgent and critical.

We cannot disciple everyone, but we can invite one special person that God seems to single out to take a journey with us. We can invest our ambitions, dreams, heart, purpose, and values in that person. If we are successful at transferring the substance of our lives into our disciples, including the vision of making disciples, then they will carry on and reproduce us and themselves in others long after we all are gone.

Disciple makers can be directed by God to come alongside specific prospective disciples who are less spiritually developed. In I Kings 19:16 God spoke to Elijah and told him it was time for him to choose a successor. He instructed Elijah exactly who to choose and where he could find him. Elijah journeyed to Shaphat, tossed his mantle on Elisha's shoulder, and invited him into a rabbi-disciple relationship.

One of the principles of the rabbi-disciple relationship is for the disciple to begin to act, think, and talk like the rabbi. This is a powerful principle in spiritual development: act like the person you want to become. Paul encouraged his disciples to imitate him as he imitated Christ (I Corinthians 11:1).

Elisha began to imitate Elijah. In fact, when Elijah was caught up in a whirlwind, Elisha picked up his mantle, returned to the river he had just crossed with his mentor, smote the water with the mantle (as he had seen Elijah do) and declared, "Where is the LORD God of Elijah?" (II Kings 2:14). By acting like the man he wanted to become, he actually performed twice as many miracles as Elijah did during his ministry.

Disciple makers see potential in their disciples. Although King Saul's son Jonathan was heir to the throne of Israel, he clearly saw the sure hand of God upon David. It sometimes goes unnoticed that Jonathan was considerably older than David. Unlike his father, Jonathan was not intimidated by David nor was he jealous of his gifting, popularity, or anointing. He chose to help David, and do what he could to prepare him for his next assignment among God's people. He invited him into a mentoring relationship, even at the risk of disappointing his father, and protected him at every opportunity.

The spirit of the disciple maker is one that earnestly desires his or her disciple to excel and to exceed. Such was the case of Barnabas who intentionally sought out the young upstart believer named Saul from Tarsus. When Saul was rejected by the church in Jerusalem (they feared his conversion was a ruse) it was Barnabas who put his own good reputation on the line and personally brought him to the church in Antioch (Acts 11:24).

It was in this local church dynamic where Saul was accepted, developed his gifts, and grew into a mighty man of God. Without the mentoring relationship with Barnabas, Saul would have never developed into such a great apostle.

Over the past few years, it has been interesting to observe the rising priority of mentoring in the corporate world. Managers have had to take on an added burden when dealing with the social complexities and dysfunctions of their employees. I hear it continually from managers that today's workers are largely lazy, unkempt, irresponsible, and unable to simply get along with one another in the workplace and with the public. Common people skills and sensibilities that were taken for granted not long ago must now be instilled in their employees while on the job.

One of the reasons for these problems is the lack of good disciple making in the home. Millions of children are being raised in dysfunctional home settings where they watch television, surf the Internet, or are otherwise left to their own devices, literally (iPad, iPhone, etc.). Millions of children have been "trained" at daycare centers and by other institutionalized supervision that cannot possibly replace the daily loving, vigilant care, and oversight of responsible and loving fathers and mothers.

The trickle-down effect of this societal reality is felt in the church. People coming to Christ in the twenty-first century lack many of the common interpersonal skills that were taken for granted a generation ago. It is not uncommon for home Bible study teachers today to also provide marriage and family counseling. Society is paying a price as it discovers that far more crimes appear to be committed behind the walls of abusive homes than in the streets.

The apostle Peter said that believers have been called "out of darkness into His marvelous light" (I Peter 2:9). Peter apparently understood that spiritual immigrants would have a challenge: they were leaving one land for another land, and leaving one culture for another culture. How much easier it is to make the transition from one kingdom to another kingdom if accompanied by a tour guide. When Jesus said, "Go make disciples," He understood that these post-sinners/pre-saints would need someone to show them the ropes, teach them the customs, and explain why we do the things we do.

The sights and sounds of an Apostolic church are familiar to those who have been around the church for some time. Conversely, outsiders in spiritual transformation can easily be distracted or discouraged from pursuing a relationship with the church. They need someone they believe in to guide them step by step.

Think about it: What if someone raised in the church all of her life suddenly found herself in a bar, casino, or a racetrack? Everything would be strange: the music, the smoke, the bartenders, the lights and noise, drunken behavior, the overall atmosphere. She would feel so out of place not knowing what was really going on, how she should act, how to get her needs met, or who to talk to if she had a question.

An Apostolic church culture is equally foreign to first-time guests. They don't understand demonstrative worship, emotional responses to the presence of God, the Spirit they are feeling, passionate preaching, or Pentecostal terminology unless someone they already know can help them interpret anything that does not make sense. We must not assume that since we are having "good church" that our guests are perfectly fine and will automatically want to return because they felt something. They could be so bewildered that they would be reluctant to return.

For those of us who have been around the church for years, or even our entire lives, try to get inside the head of a visitor or new believer. Don't you think you would have some questions about what you should do with your discretionary time and money if for many years you used to smoke, drink, do drugs, carouse, curse, and hang out in bars? Might you have some questions if all you've ever known is dull, dead, boring, ritual and liturgy, and suddenly you come into a Spirit-filled, on-fire, hand-clapping, foot-stomping, shouting, crying, tongue-talking, shake-your-hair-down church?

I heard a story about a guest who came to a Pentecostal church for the first time. He sat next to the disciple maker who invited him. He was curious and wanted an answer for every behavior he did not understand. When someone spoke in tongues, he asked about that. When a man took off running around the sanctuary, he asked what that meant. When a sister stepped out into the aisle and danced until her hair fell down, he was curious about the meaning of that. The disciple maker answered every question to the best of his ability. Then the pastor took off his watch and laid it on the pulpit as he began to preach. The guest asked what that meant. His friend replied, "Oh that doesn't mean anything."

Many visitors have come to Pentecostal churches and never returned because they had unanswered questions and left confused and befuddled. Responses by jilted Pentecostals whose guests never returned have included the assumption that they just weren't ready for the truth or perhaps not hungry enough for God. Perhaps if a disciple maker had been standing by or followed up after the service, the confused visitors could have been enlightened through a casual conversation and had their curiosity satisfied and their qualms calmed.

Another unfortunate response to this dilemma has been an attempt by some pastors to dumb down the moving of the Spirit or discourage any outburst or physical demonstration that would make anyone feel uncomfortable. This is the wrong response. A powerful Pentecostal church that is not just Spirit-thrilled but truly Spirit-filled can offer a depth of the presence of God most people have never encountered before. It is in the powerful presence of God that the invitation to find love, acceptance, deliverance, and hope for answers to the problems of life can be found. Why would anyone want to minimize that?

Too many guests have left powerful Pentecostal worship services and never returned because of the unusual behavior of total strangers. If they would have had an authentic connection with a credible person who came alongside them like a tour guide, maybe they would have returned. I taught a home Bible study to a family for seven months and never invited them to church. One night they asked me about the location of the church I served and if they visited what they could expect. I don't know why I said it but it flew out of my mouth before I could stop it, "Well, just wear your crash helmets." We shared a good laugh but I'm sure it left them wondering what I meant by that.

That next Sunday all six family members showed up for the first time at our church. Much to my chagrin everything "Pentecostal" that could happen happened. Worshipers were exuberant and demonstrative. I happened to glance back where they were sitting and their heads were swiveling back and forth like they were watching a tennis match. Unfortunately, I did not get a chance to speak with them after the service and was anxious about their observations when I saw them that next week. When I knocked on their door for the Bible study a few days later, instead of someone greeting me I heard, "Come on in, pastor." I opened the door and walked down the hallway to our usual study place in the kitchen. When I came around the corner they were all sitting at the table, and someone exclaimed, "Now!" They all simultaneously reached down under their chairs and pulled out bicycle helmets and strapped them on.

Needless to say, we had a good laugh followed by a lively discussion about their first Pentecostal worship experience. Thankfully it didn't scare them away. In fact, it made a powerful impression on them. Now, many years later, they are some of the finest members of the congregation and they engage in some of the worship behaviors they had observed during that first service. In addition, because of the model presented to them by a disciple maker, they have now turned around and have engaged others in disciple making.

Because they already had a more mature believer worth following in their lives, a person they believed in and were willing to follow, the apparent antics and unusual behaviors were not a problem. The credibility of a mature disciple maker brings assurance and confidence to the unfolding lifestyle of a new Apostolic believer.

Several years ago I preached a message I called, "Do visitors ask questions in your church?" Questions are good. Questions are healthy. It's a sign of a dysfunctional church, office, school, or family culture when people can't ask questions. And it's a sign of a dead church when people don't ask questions. The only dangerous question is one that is being answered by no one or the uninformed.

The only church Jesus ever started began on the Day of Pentecost as recorded in Acts 2. On that day in the Upper Room, things happened that no one had ever seen, felt, or heard before. There was a rushing mighty wind, divided tongues of fire, and the breakthrough phenomenon of speaking with other tongues.

When outsiders gathered around to behold this spectacle, they started asking questions: Are not all these who speak Galileans? And how is it that we hear, each in our own language? Whatever could this mean? Men and brethren what shall we do? (Acts 2:7–8, 12, 37). Apparently, the locals who were speaking with other tongues and staggering like drunks did not scare away the spectators, but actually intrigued them.

Visitors are going to have questions when they visit an authentic Pentecostal church. If there is a disciple maker in place, this should only enhance the visitors' experience and feed their spiritual hunger. (I will say more about how to put a disciple maker in place during a worship service in the last chapter.) The perceptive disciple maker understands that we live in a postmodern world. Postmoderns do not believe in absolute truth, but if you say you have truth, they respect that. However, they believe their truth is as relevant as your truth. They like stories. They believe that your story is as important as their story. They don't believe in tradition because they want something real. The exciting thing about Apostolics reaching postmoderns is that they are open to having experiences. We can offer that!

Based on this profile of our postmodern world coupled with Joel's prophecy concerning the outpouring of the Spirit in the last days, it's no wonder that over six hundred million people in the world today claim affiliation with the Charismatic or Pentecostal movements. By the year 2025 it has been projected that over one billion people will attest this affinity (Synan 2011, vii).

This phenomenon puts Pentecostals in the position of being the leaders, facilitators, teachers, models, and mentors of the greatest revival the world has ever witnessed. A great harvest is coming, spiritual birthrate is growing, and the need for disciple makers is greater than ever. We cannot afford to abort the harvest that is coming.

When sinners repent, are baptized, or filled with the Holy Ghost, they have not received a diploma but a birth certificate. They need a more mature believer to go home with them (so to speak). Not having a disciple maker in place for a new believer is like a young couple who just gave birth then wave goodbye to their newborn through the maternity glass at the hospital as if to say, "Okay little buddy, we'll see you back at the house." The command Jesus gave to go make disciples is the answer to harvesting and establishing the great end-time revival that is unfolding all around us.

A little boy woke up in the night when he heard a loud clap of thunder just outside his window. He jumped out of bed, ran into his parents' bedroom, took a flying leap, and landed right between them. His dad said, "Son, what's wrong?" The boy said, "Daddy, I heard the thunder and I got so scared I had to come into your room." His dad said, "Well, son, you know Jesus is with you in your room." He said, "I know Dad, but right now I need someone with skin on."

Disciple makers are Jesus with skin on. Let's take our disciples on a guided tour of what it means to live an overcoming, joyful, and abundant life in Christ Jesus!

Questions for discussion:

- Have you ever experienced a new place with a tour guide? Have you gone to a new place without one? What was each experience like?

- How mature do you believe a disciple must be before they can begin to make a disciple?

- What experience(s) have you had in helping someone mature in Christ and what impact did it have on you?

- What are the positive aspects of someone asking you questions about what you believe?

CHAPTER 10

THERE YOU ARE:
THE ATTITUDE
OF A DISCIPLE MAKER

When Jesus said, "Go make disciples," He was prescribing a lifestyle, a pattern, and a mentality for His followers. Jesus' personal plan to influence the generation He lived in was not to gather a large crowd once a week, but to reach just a few people by building a relationship with them on a daily basis.

There is something to be learned as we study how Jesus did the business of reaching the world. Did He send out a mass mailer with a survey and then pray over the responses? Did he make a general announcement to a large multitude inviting anyone who was interested in following Him to meet behind the stage after the meeting? Did He show an interest in inviting someone into His discipleship group only after he first showed an interest in Him? Did He make initial contact with the Twelve but then hand them off to His staff with the clichéd directive, "My people will get with your people"?

When Jesus called His disciples, He chose them intentionally and personally. In fact, after He did some initial scouting, He prayed all night long before choosing His disciples. When He called them, He did so in the rabbi-disciple motif of His culture. His invitation was offered with just two words: "Follow me."

There was something authentic, magnetic, and personable about His invitation. How else could you explain professionals leaving their careers behind on such short notice? Matthew walked away from a table full of money and four fishermen literally dropped their nets. James and John actually left their father, Zebedee, in the boat to follow Him.

Jesus was not an aloof or distant leader who was unapproachable or impossible to get close to. There are too many snapshots in Scripture to let us believe otherwise. He would have given out His phone number or email address to just about anyone. He picked up children and held them close. He touched marginalized people like the lepers and paralytics. He waited patiently for blind beggars to stumble up to Him. He allowed John to lean on His chest at the Last Supper.

John certainly felt endeared to the Master by referring to himself as the disciple whom Jesus loved (John 21:7). He even allowed Judas to come close enough to place the cold kiss of betrayal upon His cheek. All of these personal glimpses of the man Jesus present a picture of a leader who was intentional about building close relationships with the people He wanted to influence with His mission.

Jesus' model of making disciples will not only work today, but it is the tried and proven pattern of reaching the world. His method was to invite carefully chosen disciples into relationship to share His vision with them, place expectations upon them, and then release them to go and do the same with their disciples. Building relationships will always be the most effective way to reach lost people because of the deep human need to belong, be loved, and be cared for.

Fads and cultures may change, but these basic needs will never go out of style. The world has become a smaller place with the advent of the Internet and the social networking options at our fingertips. And yet there somehow seems to be an antisocial persona that is being projected on the culture. People are communicating more but talking less. We are connecting more but sitting down together less.

We pull into our driveway, press our garage door opener, and close it behind us without having to speak to anyone. We have built high privacy fences around our backyards so now we don't have to greet the neighbors when we are sitting on our back porch or cooking on the grill. Neighbors don't bond like they used to. It is not uncommon to live on a block of houses and not know anyone by name. The world is smaller in terms of connectivity and information sharing but the distance between people is greater than it's ever been. However, this dynamic is more of an opportunity than an obstacle.

It is time for the church to stop putting all of their ministry eggs in the Sunday basket and to begin distributing them all week long. Average church attendees do not live their lives Monday through Saturday with a disciple-maker mindset. Most have not yet embraced the strategy of Jesus, which was to turn sinners into friends, and friends into disciples (Matthew 11:19). The typical saved person fosters relationships only with the sanctified and not the sinners. One of the occupational hazards for mature believers is that the longer they are in the church, the less effective they typically become in reaching sinners with the gospel. We could only hope that the opposite would be true, but unfortunately such is not the case.

The most effective window of opportunity to reach sinners with a personal testimony occurs within the first few years of conversion, but we do not have to accept this reality as final. In defense of well-meaning mature saints, preachers are partially to blame for their congregants' unfruitfulness in the area of impacting outsiders. This is largely due to the great emphasis that has been placed on the call to come out of the world and to be separate. Many saints have heard such strong preaching against the world and the biblical admonition to come out of the world that they have spun themselves into a cocoon of isolation.

Being "called out" should be understood in the sense that we have been called out of a worldly attitude and lifestyle, but we have not been called away from the people that the One who called us out wants us to reach. I'm concerned that some local churches have manufactured the Rapture before its time. They have simply disappeared from the community. This is not how Christ envisioned that His church should live.

To be sure, there should be proper and balanced teaching concerning the evils that are in the world. Let us discover what God's Word means about the issues of separation but not make them something they are not. For example, Paul's prohibition of being unequally yoked together with unbelievers has to do with relationships other than a disciple-making relationship (for example, business partners or marriage).

The Lord has commanded us to "come out" (II Corinthians 6:17) but then has sent us back to reach them (John 20:21). He taught us to be like salt and light (Matthew 5:14–15). Salt must be savory and come into proximity before it is effective, and light must be turned on in darkness to be noticed. He has sent us back into the darkness after having equipped us with the light (I Peter 2:9).

The command to go make disciples is obviously not in contradiction to the call to come out of the world. Jesus' prayer in John 17:15 was, "I do not pray that You should take them out of the world, but that You should keep them from the evil one." This prayer perfectly describes the tension that exists between being in the world but not of the world. Jesus' prayer for us was not to be isolated from the world but to be insulated from the world's influence.

Jesus understood that certain risks would be incurred by sending us back into the world to make disciples after calling us out of our sinful state. He used word pictures that illustrated the irony of the work His followers must do. "Behold, I send you out as sheep in the midst of wolves. Therefore be wise as serpents and harmless as doves" (Matthew 10:16). Clearly Jesus was warning against dangers and pitfalls that potentially could destroy a believer while on the mission. He also said in Matthew 13:30 to allow the tares (weeds) and wheat to grow together and they would be separated at the time of harvest. Apparently Jesus was not too concerned about His sheep surviving among wolves or wheat becoming weeds. He was confident that He had given us power to overcome the world with the weapons He had equipped us with (Luke 10:19).

A good test of whether we are influencing those around us is to ask ourselves the question, "If the Rapture occurred today, and you were caught up to be with the Lord, would anyone left behind notice that you were gone?" This would also be a good question for a local congregation to ask themselves: "How long would it take the community our church is in to notice that we had disappeared?" Sadly, some communities would never notice that an Apostolic church had closed or was caught away. The truth is that too many good Christians have unwittingly created their own false rapture and are conducting their lives with little or no impact on people around them.

Any meaningful relationship requires intentionality for development. Many years ago as a young pastor, I desired to have an iconic preacher come and preach in our local church. I am sure he was not aware that I even existed, but I did not allow that reality to deter me. I approached him at a conference and gave him an invitation. He said he would place me on his "list." Every time I saw him at a conference over the next five years, I purposefully sought him out for a moment to remind him about my invitation. Finally one day during one of these short conversations, I asked him if I was still on his list. He said, "Yes, and you are moving up" (we shared a good laugh).

It wasn't long until he called me and we set our first meeting. He has now been coming annually to preach a conference at our church for the last seventeen years. We have become close friends and he is endeared to our family. My wife and I have stayed in his home and he has spent Thanksgiving week with us. This close relationship began with an intentional and persistent pursuit. Initially it was one-sided but now has become mutual. In fact he wrote the foreword in this book.

Jesus understood more than anyone that anything worth accomplishing in life must be pursued with intentionality. He never wasted time, words, or energy during His ministry. He daily lived out His life with purpose. Anytime Jesus directed someone to "go" in the Scriptures, the person receiving that command had every reason to get excited because something amazing was going to happen. He told the blind man to "Go wash in the pool of Siloam." He told ten lepers to "Go show yourselves to the priest." He gave the seventy power over the enemy and sent them out saying, "Go your way." He told the woman taken in the act of adultery, "Go and sin no more." When Jesus said "Go," sicknesses were healed, diseases were cured, devils were cast out, Satan fell from Heaven, and Jesus rejoiced (Luke 10:1–22). Anytime Jesus told someone to "Go," He was sending them on a miraculous journey. When the disciples heard Him say, "Go and make disciples," they well knew success would follow their action of obedience. When we arise daily to go and make disciples, we can well expect we are intentionally going on His mission, backed with all of the power of Heaven, and wonderful things are going to happen.

One reason believers are not effective in making disciples is because they don't have a disciple maker's mentality when they are around lost people. Let's see if you have a disciple maker's mentality: When you walk into a room, is your attitude best described by the phrase, "Here I am" or "There you are"? I would venture to say that when most people walk into a room, they are preoccupied with how they look, what people are thinking about them, or who they are going to be invited to sit by. The first natural assessment when we walk into a room of people is typically concern about ourselves and not others. The smallest package you will ever see is a person all wrapped up in himself or herself. Before we can go make disciples, we must have a "there you are" mentality with everyone we meet.

Jesus consistently presented a "there you are" attitude throughout His ministry. When He spoke to someone, he or she felt like the most important person in the world. He never made a ministry situation all about Him, but continually focused on others. Whether it was breaking social protocol and walking through Samaria to connect with one woman, noticing Zacchaeus perched in a tree, or turning to see who had touched Him in the midst of a crowd, Jesus always had a "there you are" attitude. When a nondescript widow gave her offering, He noticed her and talked to others about her sacrifice. Children were considered to be unimportant, but Jesus noticed them and commanded the disciples to let them come to Him.

During the six excruciating hours while hanging on the cross, He still refused to make it all about Him. Despite His agony He said things like, "Today you will be with Me in Paradise," or "Woman, behold your son," or "Father, forgive them." Even after the Resurrection He was still making His amazing appearances about others. There you are, Mary; there you are, Thomas; there you are, Peter; there you are, Cleopas. The Spirit of Christ within us enables us to be approachable and reachable by those who need what we have to offer.

Recently I preached at a conference in a state where I had served for several years as pastor of a local church and also as district youth secretary. While at this conference, we were encouraged by the person leading the service to go meet and greet someone we did not know. I randomly wandered out into the crowd and shook hands with a woman who looked vaguely familiar. When I mentioned she looked like someone I knew many years ago, she told me something that deeply touched me. She said thirty years ago as a young person she had attended a district youth event at a local church. She was sitting on the back row, all alone and very discouraged. She said that I came up to her, spoke to her, sat down beside her, and seemed to take a personal interest in her. She said she never forgot the feeling that came over her when I showed her special attention and spoke words of healing and encouragement. Since that time she has made it her mission to be on the lookout for people who are discouraged and to speak words of life into them so they can feel like she felt that night. When she told me this story, it blew me away. I have no recollection of that moment and apparently did not think much of the conversation at the time, but that attention and those few words changed her life and gave her a lifelong "there you are" mission.

Through the years my heart has been broken as I have observed Christian people who seem to be blinded to the lost people around them. I have witnessed them being rude to employees in restaurants. I have watched them in amazement as they become belligerent with hotel employees. I have actually given additional tips to table servers who ran themselves ragged, were treated rudely, and were left a meager tip. Many years ago I gave a ministry position to someone at our local church. One day I noticed that person walk right by a group of people in our lobby without smiling, making eye contact, or stopping to shake their hands. I followed the person until we could speak in private and asked, "What are you called to do?" The reply was, "I'm called into the ministry." I said, "Well you just flunked your first test because you walked right by your job."

A long time ago I heard a conference speaker admonish all the ministers to "walk slowly through the crowd." I have tried to do this consistently as a pastor. For a short time, I was on staff at a small church. An evangelist had come through years before and apparently rebuked the church because they failed to stand up when their pastor walked into the sanctuary. So from that day forward, when the music started, the pastor would come busting out of his office from the back corner of the sanctuary and, on cue, the congregation would rise to their feet. His rapid gait was matched by the two or three service leaders as they fell in line and made their way to the platform. The first time I witnessed this anomaly I was shocked and thought for sure the band was going to begin playing, "Hail to the Chief."

Show me a pastor who goes from the church parking lot directly to the church office to the platform for service and then directly back to the church office without spending any time greeting anybody, and I'll show you a congregation without any warmth, depth, or hospitality. For years I have walked slowly through the crowd during the worship time just connecting with guests, shaking hands, hugging old ladies, kissing babies, touching children, praying many ten-second prayers, and just loving people. Although I should warn you that I have also been ambushed a few times.

Before I ascend to the platform I have always felt as though I wanted to smell like sheep, be among the flock of God, feel their hurts, pray over their pain, and hear their concerns. I never want to become a lab coat technician behind the pulpit but rather, one among equals. Ministers and pastors should take their cue from Jesus, who though He was our High Priest, was confronted with all of our temptations (Hebrews 4:15). Jesus walked slowly through the crowd.

Every member of a local church should have a disciple maker's "there you are" attitude, not only when they are out in public, but also when they are at a worship service. I recently heard about someone who visited a large congregation, arrived on time, and left after the altar call, and not one person acknowledged that person's presence. I would think with a congregational personality like this that any sermon about reaching lost people and making disciples would sound empty. Good church members can become moved about fulfilling the mission of Christ and still inexplicably allow guests (who are their hottest leads) to leave without ever greeting them with a "there you are" welcome (much less engaging them in a meaningful conversation).

The average congregation would never need to knock a door or send out a mass mailer and still grow by five percent per year if they would make sure to intentionally make disciples out of the precious guests who walk in on any given Sunday. Show me a hospitality team and a congregation full of "there you are" disciple makers and I'll show you a redemptive organism that is making a significant impact on their local community for Christ.

Questions for discussion:

* How has our culture hindered or helped in making disciples?

* Who do you know who possesses a "there you are" spirit?

* What does the phrase "walk slowly through the crowd" communicate to you?

CHAPTER 11

UNLIKELY DISCIPLE MAKERS OF THE BIBLE:
THERE ARE NO EXCUSES

In this chapter I will attempt to deconstruct some of the excuses routinely employed by well-meaning born-again believers to either disqualify or exempt themselves from the call of Christ upon their lives to go make disciples. Some of the excuses I have heard through the years have been pretty creative, sometimes elaborate, and nearly convincing. In fact, a few folks have almost had me persuaded that Jesus gave them a special dispensation and never intended for the Great Commission to apply to them.

In chapter 8 I mentioned the congregation that had not seen a baptism in two years and in our first three months there, by the grace of God, we baptized sixteen. I was excited and assumed that everyone else would be too. There was one man in the church who did not like all these new people coming into church with all their hang-ups and problems. In his mind they were messing up his nice little church and upsetting his theological applecart. When I told him that he could teach a Bible study to a sinner, he actually said to me, "Well, Jeremiah never won a soul."

This was his pitiful response to my vision of reaching our community for Christ. I didn't have the time or patience right then to give him a dispensational overview of Scripture or to inform him that he was carnal, rebellious, lukewarm, and making God sick. Other than that he was a pretty nice guy.

Here is a popular and spiritual-sounding excuse for not making disciples: "We send missionaries to make disciples of all nations. We pay and they pray. We give and they go. We spend and then send. They have the missionary gift, not me." In fact, more than ever before, it should be obvious that the Great Commission to make disciples of all nations was given to every single believer in the twenty-first century. Consider the multiculturalism prevalent throughout much of North America. We don't have to sail the seven seas to make disciples in other nations. The nations have sailed to us and have moored their vessels right at the dock of our back doors.

When it comes to the mandate to make disciples, some mature believers don't feel qualified to do so despite the fact they have been soaking in the sanctuary for years. On the contrary, I believe that every born-again believer is qualified to make a disciple. Regrettably, the more mature some people become in Christ, the less effective they are in making disciples. Most people who influence their friends and family to follow Christ do so within a short time of their initial conversion. They eventually learn to sit back, relax, and enjoy good church services with the rest of the content congregation who have exempted themselves from the responsibility and privilege of disciple making.

Don't wait to have the answers to all of life's questions before you decide to become a disciple maker. Don't wait until you know the answer to every Bible question. Don't wait until you have perfected Christianity in your personal life. Don't wait until you upgrade yourself to something more for God than you are now. Don't wait until God speaks to you personally about making disciples.

If you still feel unqualified to be a disciple maker, consider the first disciples. How qualified were they to make disciples? They were not chosen from the hallowed halls of universities. Jesus may have hoped that His followers smelled more like heavenly phosphorus and less like mud and dead fish. Their lack of education and career choices like fishing, tax collecting, and active rebellion against the Romans did not exactly earn them first-round draft choice status by recruiting rabbis.

Don't forget that Jesus only spent forty-two months with them, and then He physically left them—permanently. In addition, they did not have the advantage of the New Testament writings at their fingertips. Neither did they have dedicated meeting places where they could continue to learn, teach, and train. Transportation was not easy for them. Most of their travel was on foot and much of the land they traversed was rocky and hilly. They lacked many of the advantages that we commonly enjoy and yet seemed to do much more with much less.

Surely today's disciple makers can be as effective as Jesus' disciples in making disciples. We have the completed Word of God, much easier and faster methods of travel, and a multitude of resources including books, DVDs, podcasts, and so on. We are blessed with thousands of local congregations being served by dedicated pastors and teachers who continually feed and train the flock of God.

Jesus' unlikely cast of disciples were equipped, empowered, and engaged to fulfill their Savior's prophesied destiny. Thirty years after the church was born, Paul demonstrated that the disciple-making culture was yet ensconced in the psyche and performance of the church. He wrote to Timothy, his disciple, and said, "And the things that you have heard from me among many witnesses, commit these to faithful men who will be able to teach others also" (II Timothy 2:2). Contained within this solitary verse is Paul's vision of four generations of disciple making. Paul fully expected that Timothy would teach faithful men, and that those men would, in turn, make disciples of many others.

Let's take a look at a few unlikely disciple makers whose stories are provided for us in Scripture. The narrative of Naomi's life is one of regret, loss, and grief. She and her husband and two sons left Bethel during a famine and came to live in Moab. While there, her two sons married Moabite women named Ruth and Orpah. It wasn't long until she suffered the death of her husband and her two sons. A lesser woman may have grieved herself to an untimely death.

When she heard that the famine was over in Bethel, she announced her decision to return. The Bible says that Orpah kissed her and stayed in Moab while Ruth clave to her and insisted on going back with her. When Naomi arrived in Bethel, she was greeted by name. Her reply is noteworthy: "But she said to them, 'Do not call me Naomi; call me Mara, for the Almighty has dealt very bitterly with me. I went out full, and the Lord has brought me home again empty. Why do you call me Naomi, since the Lord has testified against me, and the Almighty has afflicted me?'" (Ruth 1:20–21). You can hear the despondency in her tragic summary and the end result of her time away from the house of God.

What amazes me in this story is that with all of Naomi's brokenness, Ruth still desired to follow her. Despite her haggard outlook, frazzled spirit, and extreme grief and bitterness of heart, Ruth somehow still caught a glimpse of something in Naomi that captured her heart. Ruth could see past the pain and regret of Naomi's life to the extent that she was willing to pull up stakes, leave her own family, and journey to a strange land with no promise of a bright future.

Of course we know the rest of the story, which we will not take time to comment on here. But I am arrested by the fact that despite Naomi's limited and even tainted presentation to Ruth, this heathen woman still would not let her go. Naomi was far from presenting her best, yet a residue of God's grace lingered in her so much so that Ruth desired whatever she had for her own life. Little did Ruth know what wonderful and transformational events awaited her in Bethel.

I grew up with an outstanding young man who graduated from Bible school. Within a short time, his heart became discouraged concerning ministry and his chosen path led him away from a faithful walk with God. He worked with an unsaved man for some time and they developed a close friendship. This man was hungry and looking for God. During the course of several conversations, the backslider turned to his friend and said, "Well, if you want to find God and get saved, I can tell you what church you need to go to." He directed him to my home church, where he visited and soon made a decision to give his life to Christ. It wasn't long until he was baptized in water and in the Spirit. Now many years later, after church planting and serving as a career missionary, he leads a thriving church in North America. Despite his backslider friend's own failures, he still could see enough light in him to be attracted to what he had forsaken.

I'm sure you get the message. Our worst day walking with God is better than our best day without Him. A born-again believer has more of the light of Jesus Christ in the tip of his or her little finger than what someone in the world has ever seen. We must not sell ourselves short of what emanates out of us, even when we are not operating at a high level.

Many times I have sat across a table from a prospective believer and was so exhausted that I felt I had nothing to give. I have literally felt as though I was wasting our time due to my less-than-stellar attitude or spiritual condition. And yet, by the grace of God, the Word still penetrated that person's heart. Amazingly, the longer the discussion went concerning the Lord and His Word, the more energized I became.

I think this may have something to do with Jesus' response to the disciples' question when they came back to the well of Samaria and found Him energized. He sent them away to get food as He sat wearily on the well. His answer to their question regarding His mysterious energy source was, "I have food to eat of which you do not know" (John 4:32).

The effectiveness of the Word of God in a disciple-making context is not predicated upon the skillfulness or condition of the sower. In the parable of the Sower, the Seed, and the Soil (Matthew 13), the seed was disseminated indiscriminately. The seed that fell on good (hungry) ground sprung up and was fruitful, regardless of the skill or condition of the sower.

There are going to be opportunities for us to make disciples out of people who may be headed for greater things than we ourselves. To be sure, there will come a time when they will pass us by in every way, and at that point we may hand them off to someone more equipped. However, we should not disqualify ourselves from leading a potentially more gifted disciple. Although this seems unlikely, it can, at least initially, be effective.

For example, would there have ever been an apostle Paul had it not been for Barnabas? I think not. Acts 9:26 says that the new convert Saul tried to join the disciples in Jerusalem but was rejected. It took the disciple-making diligence of Barnabas to track him down in Tarsus and take him to Antioch before Saul would become accepted among the believers anywhere.

Early on in the narrative between this disciple maker and his disciple, the Scripture refers to this combination as "Barnabas and Saul." The list of the Antioch prophets and teachers (Acts 13:1) is headed up by Barnabas, but Saul is mentioned last (at least he made the cut). But something happened between Acts 13:7 (Barnabas and Saul) and verse 43 (Paul and Barnabas). Paul's gifts, anointing, and leadership ability surpassed his mentor and this transition is noted subtly in the narrative.

Barnabas had the true spirit of a teacher. Any called teacher would want his or her students to exceed him or her. It would be a dysfunctional, insecure, and controlling teacher who would not want his or her students to excel and go beyond. Barnabas was not threatened or intimidated by Paul's growth and development. I don't think Barnabas hunted Luke down and complained that he was no longer given top billing. In fact, I'm sure that he celebrated Paul's accomplishments, of course giving all glory to God, but also taking satisfaction in the fact that he played a part in Paul's foundational development.

Jesus certainly was not an unlikely disciple maker but He demonstrated the true spirit of a teacher (there was none greater) when He envisioned the future for His disciples. At such a moment He said, "Most assuredly, I say to you, he who believes in Me, the works that I do he will do also; and greater works than these he will do, because I go to My Father" (John 14:12).

It's a wonderful thing when the disciple believes in the disciple maker, but it's more wonderful when the disciple maker believes in the disciple. I have discovered throughout my years of serving as a pastor and working with new believers that the utmost cry of nearly every heart is for someone to believe in them. Any local church that is "others" oriented, invests time in their new believers, equips and empowers them, and believes in them will be a growing, revival church.

No followers of Jesus Christ, newborn or mature, should ever exempt or disqualify themselves from making disciples. A slave girl told a captain in the Syrian army (who had undoubtedly persecuted her parents) about a prophet that could tell him how to be healed. It was mild-mannered Andrew who introduced his boisterous and impulsive brother, Peter, to the Master. Jonathan, despite the fact he was heir to the throne, recognized the anointing upon David's life and preferred him and helped prepare him to lead the nation of Israel. Apollos was more naturally gifted and perhaps more anointed than Aquila and Priscilla but that didn't stop them from taking him aside and investing in his future.

Every disciple maker is going to be flawed. We are all the product of a broken world. We should not feel that we must master every aspect of walking with God before we enter the world of making disciples. If preachers wait to preach a sermon until they have perfected every aspect of it in their personal lives, there will be a lot of great preaching that will never get done. That's not to say that we should become cavalier about embodying Scripture or become content with hypocrisy in the pulpit. If preaching is not real, then it doesn't help anyone. The same principle applies in disciple making. If disciple makers are not authentic, not living in a real world, not sharing some of their battles and struggles and how they overcame, then there will be little or no connection with their disciple. Disciple makers should share their stories of temptations, battles, and struggles and how they have processed defeat and celebrated victory.

There is a big difference between projecting an image and projecting reality. To be sure, if we truly let our disciples into our lives, they will perhaps notice some of our humanity and weaknesses. This may not be such a bad thing. One of the worst things we could do is to project absolute perfection before our disciples. This would be unfortunate not only because it is not the real picture, but this perception may also discourage them from even trying. I am not advocating the airing of all our dirty laundry before our disciples, but neither should we remove all hope of them ever growing in Christ because we pretended to have achieved the illusive level of sinless perfection.

Jesus was the greatest disciple maker that the world has ever seen. He came down to the level of the unlikely followers He had chosen. How real did He need to be with them? Had He continually talked only about His sinless life, His perfection, and all the things He was that they were not, how discouraging would that have been for His followers? Although He was the perfect Son of God, He carried that glory in such a way as to attract and inspire His followers to want to believe in Him.

Jesus kept it real. He laughed, cried, hungered, thirsted, and grew weary. He hugged children, demonstrated care for the marginalized, touched lepers, and fed hungry people. It's no small wonder that His disciples emulated Him to the point that outsiders remarked how obvious it was that they had spent time with Him (Acts 4:13). Jesus so inspired His disciples with His authentic leadership that they were all willing to lay down their lives for Him.

Ultimately, Jesus saved nothing for Himself but gave everything away. He gave away His authority, His principles, His prime years, His hope of starting a family, His energy, His blood, His back, His brow, His face, His hands, His feet, and His side. Most of all, He gave away His power. The power that all believers receive at the infilling of the Holy Spirit is the power of Jesus Christ to be witnesses (Acts 1:8) or to make disciples. We can do no less for our disciples, and that is to give everything we have, including our power, away. Making a disciple is the only way to fulfill the Great Commission. Let's stop making excuses and start making disciples.

Questions for discussion:

- What would you tell someone who feels unqualified or uncalled to make a disciple?

- What inadequacies in a Bible character encourage you about being a disciple maker?

- What is the fine line between being real with our disciple(s) but not necessarily revealing every weakness or private thoughts we deal with in our lives?

CHAPTER 12

MAKE A DISCIPLE, SECURE THE FUTURE:

DISCIPLING

THE NEXT GENERATION

One of the most compelling motivations to make disciples is to secure the future. The daily demands of disciple making can be so great that we lose sight of the bigger picture. Obviously we want sinners to be saved and become fruitful believers who then turn around and make disciples, but there is a bigger issue at stake: the preservation of a culture. When a species fails to reproduce itself, it will be lost in one generation. Countless animal and plant species have become extinct to the ages, as well as many human cultures, because of a failure to reproduce.

The Oneness Pentecostal movement as we know it today is constantly one generation from extinction. Many religious organizations born in the red hot fires of revival with a move of God demonstrated by miracles, wonders, and signs have now cooled and calmed themselves into spiritual mediocrity. Few, if any, characteristics remain from their early years of coming to birth. I have lived long enough to have watched many believers walk away from Apostolic truth. In my years as a saint, licensed minister, pastor, and district and national leader, I have grieved as I have watched individuals, families, ministers, pastors, congregations, and entire organizations depart from their formerly-held Apostolic beliefs. I completely understand that there is no possible way to guarantee the longevity of Oneness Pentecostalism in any one individual, but there is a way to preserve the truth as we know it today in a family, a congregation, and a movement: Go make disciples!

I am of the opinion that a believer who is willing to be truly discipled will never depart from the faith. I am not suggesting the false doctrine of eternal security when I say this. I know that saying true disciples will not backslide may sound like false doctrine, and may even border on sounding judgmental. That is not my intention. I understand that parents cannot guarantee that their children will grow up to become adults that continue to hold the values of their parents. James Dobson said that you never know how well you instilled your values within your children until you observe your grandchildren.

A few years ago I organized a reunion of my former junior high boys Sunday school class. All of us were raised by faithful parents and our pastor was one of the greatest teachers of the last century. I was heartbroken to discover that out of the ten of us present, perhaps only three were yet committed to Oneness Pentecostal beliefs. This tragic scenario has been repeated countless times around the country and may even be your own testimony. Where did it go wrong? The parents? The children? The local church? There is no easy answer to such a painful question. The simple fact is that somewhere there was a breakdown in the process of making a disciple, because disciples last.

The apostle John wrote, "They went out from us, but they were not of us; for if they had been of us, they would have continued with us; but they went out that they might be made manifest, that none of them were of us" (I John 2:19). John said that those who left them were never of them. Then he appeared to make his point even more obvious when he said that they would not have left had they ever been part of them.

Who were these people? Obviously they initially manifested some brand of Christianity, but somehow never became true disciples of the apostles' faith. They worshiped with them, fellowshiped with them, and apparently served the Lord in some capacity with them, but they did not stay because they never received the spiritual DNA of the apostles' faith. John told his readers that they were different than those who left because they had received the Spirit and knew the truth. Of course the question remains: could something have been done to make them true disciples? Certainly, either on their part or on the part of the apostles and other saints. But had they become disciples, they would not have left.

When we make disciples who are truly of us (like us, imitators of us), we should expect that they will not leave us. (See I Corinthians 11:1.) Some that leave the faith apparently never were true disciples. Jesus said that He kept all of His disciples with the exception of Judas (John 17:12). Even Jesus experienced the disappointment of one that chose not to follow Him. But His retention rate of 92 percent is better than most. What is your retention rate?

Whenever I am given the opportunity to speak with young people or ministers I try to tell them what I believe to be a simple formula for remaining true to the truth. First of all, it is imperative to love the truth. Remember that truth is a person before it is a fact. Jesus said, "I am the . . . truth" (John 14:6). How does one know if he or she loves the truth? You will know you love the truth when it excites you while hearing it preached or taught. You will know you love the truth when a tear is brought to your eyes while reading the Word of God or celebrating planks of truth in prayer unto God. You will know you love the truth when someone attacks the truth in your presence and it incites a passionate response from you.

Paul said that some would not receive the love of the truth (II Thessalonians 2:10). If this is the case, then he said they would become a candidate to receive a strong delusion (from God) and would become capable of believing a lie. I have heard people trumpet their new revelation (something heretofore they condemned) and say they received it from the Lord. If this revelation came as a result of failing to receive a love of the truth, then in fact they did receive their revelation from God. In such a case, deception feels just like revelation because they both came from God. Loving the truth safeguards us against deception.

Second, it is of primary importance that the younger generation connects with elders. One observation I have is that millennials tend to share their thoughts, ideas, and feelings primarily with their own generation. This phenomenon has been facilitated largely by the advent of social media. While it is normal and logical to synthesize life within your own demographic, it is critical to have the voice of elders, not only for direction and wisdom, but also for the safety of veto privileges and opportunities for promotion. It is my observation that every ministry that has been singularly blessed by God, without exception, includes a prolific component of honoring elders. Some people I have admired through the years and have heard deliver a message on many occasions cannot seem to do so without giving great respect and honor to the shapers and mentors of their ministry. Any life or ministry without the covering and protection of the older generation will typically lack depth and maturity. Connect with elders.

Third, the preservation of Apostolic integrity requires moral purity. Your morality will dictate your theology. Although it is not so across the board, in some cases where individuals have departed from the truth it has been the accumulative result of hidden sin in their lives. In fact, some former Apostolic pastors have announced to their congregations that they were taking them in a new direction only to discover later that immorality had been present either in them or widespread within the congregation for quite some time. I have yet to hear someone say that after coming off a twenty-one day fast, God distinctly spoke to them about throwing away Apostolic identity and that separation from the world is no longer necessary. Departing from the Oneness Pentecostal faith is often framed within a context of revelation, freedom, liberty, or even deliverance, but it has never had anything to do with these things. The usual reason for departing from the faith is typically carnality and not spirituality.

The lack of maintaining Apostolic truth and identity reveals the absence of authentic disciple making. We need not lose one more young person, one more family, one more minister, one more local congregation, or one more organization to something other than Oneness Pentecostalism. I recently attended a revival-type conference where the age demographics were diverse. I could not help but notice one nineteen-year-old man who was dressed sharply, presented himself well, and stood out as eager to hear the Word preached and to be in the presence of God. I discovered that he loves Apostolic truth and has brought numerous young men from the local university he attends to his local church. Many times his father has left the church late at night while this young man stayed to pray. He carries a humble presence but with a strong anointing. Where did he acquire such values? How did he achieve such a commitment to Apostolic doctrine, lifestyle, and a desire to make disciples? Did he just fall off the turnip truck in the parking lot of this conference? Oh no, his parents were intentional and made a disciple out of him from the time he was a child. I am certain that he will be heard from in his generation. He embodies the three dynamics addressed earlier: love of truth, respect for elders, and keeping sin out of his life. This is a prescription for perpetuating Apostolic greatness.

One of the obvious requirements of making a lasting disciple is to possess spiritual DNA of authentic Oneness Pentecostalism. Jesus said that the disciples of the Pharisees were doubly the children of Hell (Matthew 23:15). They reproduced in their disciples the spiritual DNA of their own destiny. Disciple makers must examine their hearts, actions, motives, character, and ambitions to ensure they have the capability of reproducing authentic Apostolic practice in their disciples. As we have emphasized in another chapter, it does not require Christlike perfection to make a disciple. The greatest attribute of a disciple maker is to be real. The effectiveness of a disciple maker is incrementally reduced when there is hypocrisy, a lack of integrity, or an absence of authenticity. When the prospective disciple observes these character flaws, the result will be a loss of respect. The closer you get to someone, the more humanity it is possible to see. Authentic disciple makers, however, actually look better the closer you get to them. Closeness may reveal warts, blemishes, and freckles, but if the character is pristine and if the Holy Spirit is operating within, the disciple will not become discouraged.

My parents secured the Apostolic future in our family for my generation by making disciples out of my brother, my two sisters, and me. At my parents' fiftieth wedding anniversary in 1993, I, along with my three siblings and our children, gathered around them and began to verbally bless them. We thanked them for staying together, loving God passionately, raising us to love the truth, and modeling the behavior they desired to see reproduced in us. When we asked them what they did to make disciples out of us, they seemed somewhat at a loss for answers, but I can tell you what they did. They had prayer lives, they never debated whether or not we were going to church, we had family altar once a week; they were parents who were present in our lives. We would catch them praying or reading the Bible; we never heard them speak disparagingly against other Christians, the church, or leadership. They were the real deal, not fake. They behaved exactly the same in public as they did at home.

Although Dad was a full-time minister while serving as teacher at a Bible college and on the local church pastoral staff, we never felt as though his calling was a hazard to our overall spiritual health. We never felt as though we had to play second fiddle to his first love being the ministry or some other interest. Shortly before my father passed away, I had a private moment with him where I knelt in front of him and promised him that I would be faithful to the values that he instilled in me. I can speak for my own children who are all adults now and say that the discipleship values he instilled in me are now present in them. Paul wrote to Timothy and said, "When I call to remembrance the genuine faith that is in you, which dwelt first in your grandmother Lois and your mother Eunice, and I am persuaded is in you also" (II Timothy 1:5). This is the ideal for how disciple making should work within families. Parents should be intentional disciple makers first of all to their children.

Other religions and culture groups understand the power of making disciples out of their children. Muslims, Roman Catholics, Amish, and other groups have developed strong methods of ensuring children do not depart from their parents' beliefs. In some groups or cultures, if one leaves the faith, he or she may face disinheritance, shunning, or even physical harm. Reaching children at a young age is especially important. Children are purposefully and systematically indoctrinated under strict religious rules or in specialized schools. For many groups, their method of growth has relied heavily on their success in making disciples of children.

Jesus secured the future when He made disciples. I shudder to think where the church would be today had He not done so (as opposed to only spending time with the multitude). Jesus knew that He had to reproduce Himself in twelve men and pass on to them His spiritual DNA so that nothing would be lost when He went away. Maybe they didn't do absolutely everything 100 percent the way He would have done it if somehow He could have continued to direct them physically on earth. Does He always get His perfect way among us? The Scripture is clear that the church is built upon the foundation of the apostles and prophets, and Jesus Christ is the chief cornerstone (Ephesians 2:20). This means that the foundational stones of the apostles were consistent with the original stone, not in preeminence but in kind.

Judas fell short of becoming a true disciple of Jesus, but the other men that Jesus personally discipled not only resembled Him in their ministry (Acts 4:13), but made the ultimate sacrifice by laying down their lives as He did. (John apparently escaped martyrdom miraculously and apparently did not taste death as prophesied by Jesus, and some believe he was taken up much like Enoch and Elijah. See Luke 9:27.) The disciples not only carried on the work of taking the gospel to the whole world, but they also continued the method of doing so by making disciples. They did not design some new, revolutionary way to reach lost people, but faithfully continued in the "Go make disciples" pattern established by Jesus. We know this because of the disciple-making language that bleeds through their writings in the epistles (as referenced in some detail in other chapters).

One of the saddest verses in the Bible is Judges 2:10, "And also all that generation were gathered unto their fathers, and there arose another generation after them, which knew not the LORD, nor yet the works which he had done for Israel." God took Moses aside and invested His truth and power in him. Moses took Joshua aside and made a disciple out of him, leaving the Israelites in capable hands when he died. Moses brought them through the wilderness and Joshua brought them into the Promised Land. But this verse describes a bleak condition that sent Israel into the dark and oppressive period of the Judges. Could it be that Joshua made no disciple? Freedom is never won conclusively, but every generation must fight for it. We cannot risk losing ground by failing to make disciples.

While in college Dr. James Dobson's goal was to become the school's tennis champion. When he won the tournament, he was elated that his trophy was prominently displayed in the school's trophy cabinet. Many years later someone mailed his trophy to him. They included a note that said they were doing some renovations and found his prized trophy in a trash can. My friends, given enough time, all of our trophies will end up in someone's trash can. How many of us could recall our own great grandparents' first names right now? How long will it take for your descendants to forget you? Within a few generations you will be completely forgotten. This is why we must make disciples during our lifetime.

Who is your disciple that you are investing in to make sure that when you are gone that your Apostolic DNA will remain on this earth? Pastor, who are you training now to succeed you, thus ensuring that your years of labor will not be destroyed by a non-disciple? Dad and Mom, do not let your faith and values be lost in the lives of your children. If they have strayed from the faith, then go make disciples of sinners and adopt spiritual children to carry on your precious Apostolic life (of course never stop praying for your own children to come back to truth). Make a disciple; secure the future.

Questions for discussion:

- Why is connecting with elders a significant part of faithfully walking in truth?

- How can entertaining sin in your personal life affect your theology?

- How does up-close authentic Christianity enhance disciple making?

CHAPTER 13

WHERE DO WE GO FROM HERE?

PRACTICAL MINISTRY APPLICATIONS FOR MAKING DISCIPLES

The church has an unprecedented opportunity to provide training to people today. Many who are coming out of the world do not have the advantage of having been raised in a nuclear family with a biblical worldview. They may lack common people skills, the ability to build relationships, or struggle knowing how to raise and disciple their own children. Some people are lazy, show up for work late (if they have a job), leave early, take lengthy breaks, or steal from the company they work for. The normal skills that people were taught as children a generation ago are generally nonexistent today. Disciple making may involve more than just presenting the gospel and a pattern of godly living. People in today's culture often need up-close models of decency, honesty, a strong work ethic, and people skills. The world needs disciple makers.

Most of the pastors I know, including myself, are bottom-line type leaders. We want to get to the pragmatic points of any discussion or idea. If I was reading this book I'm sure that I would be asking myself questions such as, "Okay, I get it. Now what practical measures can we take to make disciples as a congregation? How does making disciples fit into a local church structure that already has well-oiled programs? If disciple making is truly organic, then what does that look like in a practical sense on a personal level?"

Through the years, when I have been asked questions about the ministry or church work in general, I have typically given my opinion but then have been quick to add that I was not ready to write my book on the subject. Well, I guess I can't say that any longer. However, I still don't feel as though I have all the answers. The ideas presented below are a few of the things we are currently doing that may inspire a thought or idea you can use or incorporate in your worship setting. Hopefully you can take whatever we may be doing and make it better. The possibilities are unlimited!

Programs versus Making Disciples

A local church with good programs and ministries that also has a desire to make disciples does not need to throw away what they are already doing to reach people. Local church ministries and disciple making are not in competition but are complementary. It's not an either/or but a both/and partnership. If the vision of the church is to reach the community with the gospel, then every ministry director/leader should have in his or her heart a desire to make disciples through the ministry. I am of the opinion that no ministry is exempt from or incapable of having at least some component of disciple making. This is the only business of the church that our Founder assigned us to do!

Every ministry in the local church should have the overarching purpose of making disciples. Unfortunately, a great percentage of the ministry of the average congregation is maintenance focused rather than discipleship focused. I would venture a guess that 90 percent of the average church budget, calendar, human resources, and ministry efforts are dedicated to taking the water to the sea while precious little goes to the desert. However, Jesus called us to be fishers of men, not keepers of the aquariums.

Some of the ministries that our church operates are: Men, Ladies, Children, Student, Hyphen, Multicultural, Global Missions, Hospitality, Altar, Baptismal, Home Bible Studies, Bus, Ministerial Training, and a few others. The good news is that a disciple-making component can complement virtually every ministry that you have already engaged. In fact, if there is a ministry that is not about reaching lost people or affecting spiritual transformation, I'm not sure why any church would waste time and resources with it.

Men's and Ladies' Ministries

The men's and ladies' ministries in our local church have disciple-making (or mentoring) components. For example, the men have various small disciple-making groups that meet weekly in public locations (typically fast-food restaurants). These groups may consist of three to seven men, with one or two of them more mature and the others a work of grace in progress. The ladies have regular mentoring meetings called "Titus 2." (See Titus 2:3–5, where Paul presented the vision of the older women teaching the younger.) These meetings always have a spiritual impartation segment but they also include some practical aspect of training, such as raising children, cooking, hairstyling, sewing, hospitality, controlling the atmosphere of their home, and so on.

Children's Ministry

Children are not too young to make disciples. There is no reason why grade-school-age children cannot begin making disciples out of their friends this early in life. Our children's pastor caught the disciple-making vision and challenged the children to teach Bible studies to their friends. They used a study designed for children and their friends. Within a few weeks they had collectively taught seventy-eight Bible studies with some positive results. Some of the children taught their friends along with their friends' parents. Young disciple makers grow up to become adult disciple makers.

360 Groups

For twenty-five years we offered small group ministry to our church members. The original vision of our small groups was to lower the threshold of exposure to Pentecost by inviting guests into homes. Our thinking was that guests could come into a relaxed atmosphere, make friends, experience the presence of God, and then naturally want to come to church. Our vision was that small groups would provide opportunities for prayer, fellowship, discipleship, and accountability. We wanted to meet the needs of the body of Christ on the lowest level possible, but also to expose our neighborhoods to what the church had to offer, in local neighborhoods on a smaller scale.

Our small groups (Home Fellowship Groups) provided some accountability, and they did meet many emotional, physical, and spiritual needs (food, clothing, support, hospital visitation, and so forth). While our groups failed to become the front door of the church to lost people, they did seem to help us close the back door and establish new believers. Our groups eventually became care groups, where we met the needs of saved and sanctified people but without much vision for "neighbors." Over a period of a few years the momentum of our groups waned and proved Proverbs 29:18 to be true once again: "Where there is no vision, the people perish" (KJV). This was not such a bad thing, however, because we had already begun casting vision to make disciples and needed a new small group paradigm.

One of the concepts that seemed to take pressure off of well-meaning people who were not confident in their personal ability to "turn the world upside down" was when we began to communicate that in the realm of disciple making, less is more. After we let our small groups die, we started smaller small groups. We call these "360 groups," which communicates the idea of coming full circle. We believe that a disciple is not fully discipled until they go full circle and turn around and begin to make a disciple (and even after they begin that process they may yet need continued discipling). A 360 group consists of not less than two but not more than five people, with one or two being disciple makers and two to three disciples. Their only criteria to qualify as a 360 group is they must meet weekly (the location is unimportant) and they must function within a teaching/sharing/accountability format.

We currently have three times as many 360 groups as we had home fellowship groups. We have not encumbered these groups with layers of paperwork or administrative red tape. We want disciple making to be as organic as possible, but certainly with a sense of accountability to the local church and our discipleship pastor. One way we accomplish this is by keeping the vision alive through weekly testimonies that are shared on Sundays via video. I cannot tell you how moving these presentations are. The testimony blesses everyone: the one who shared it, the disciple or disciple maker, the families of all these people, and the congregation. As a side benefit, someone may be sitting out there thinking, "Man, if he or she can make a disciple, I know for sure I can."

One thing I have discovered as a pastor is that vision "leaks." Like a slow-leaking tire that needs to be continually aired up, a congregation needs to have the pastor's vision continually brought before them (every thirty days is the optimum). We can't expect the saints we lead to stay inspired and still committed to a vision in August that we cast with one brilliant sermon back in January, but haven't said a word about it since. We have been on a disciple-making journey for over three years and not until recently did I actually have a strong sense that we were changing the culture of the church and truly becoming a disciple-making congregation. It has been a wonderful, life-changing, congregation-changing journey, but it does take some time to turn a ship around.

You can either have a church that has a disciple-making ministry or you can become a disciple-making church. The difference is that in the former case, a few people on a ministry team are the only disciple makers in the congregation, and everyone knows that is their job, but they themselves are not expected to participate. Or, you can have every ministry committed to making disciples and every mature believer being able to answer the question, "Who is your disciple?" The quickest path to becoming a disciple-making church is for the pastor and staff to model disciple-making behavior, reveal their disciples, and tell their stories.

Baptismal Ministry

The baptismal ministry has taken on new significance since we committed to making disciples. Previously the baptismal team gave candidates a short orientation about what to expect during their baptism followed by a presentation of a baptismal certificate afterwards. However, after discovering the desperate need to make disciples rather than just win souls, we decided that we would not just send them home with a certificate but also with a disciple maker. In fact, we decided that we would not baptize anyone unless there was a disciple maker either already in their lives (not by their estimation but ours) or we would assign one to them.

We now have a fairly large pool of disciple makers we can assign to baptismal ministry on any given Sunday. These folks are present at the orientation and also when they receive their certificate. Baptism recipients are sent home with the understanding that we are committed to their spiritual development and that someone is going to be teaching them a Bible study beginning that week. We do our best to pair each new believer with geographic and demographic considerations.

Shepherd's Staff

You never get a second chance to make a good first impression on your church guests. The visitors who walk through your doors on any given Sunday are the hottest leads you have to make disciples. Like most churches, we have a hospitality team that welcomes guests from the parking lot, through the lobby, and into the sanctuary. They are available to take guests to areas of interest or need and to answer questions. I'm not sure if you have ever thought about the hospitality team as disciple makers, but the journey of spiritual transformation can begin in the parking lot. The first impressions people need to have are the best smiles and attitudes of everyone in the congregation. Guests will make a decision whether or not they are going to visit your church again long before the choir sings or the pastor preaches an amazing message. (Some research says that decision is made within eleven minutes after driving on the campus.)

Beyond the hospitality team, we have a disciple-making ministry we call The Shepherd's Staff. They are commissioned with the responsibility of guest services inside the worship space. We have assigned a shepherd and his or her team over each of the six sections of seating in the sanctuary. Their primary ministry is to make a spiritual connection with each guest. They welcome guests, help them find a seat (if necessary), and discreetly observe them throughout the service. When the altar call is given, if the guest comes forward, they gently come alongside, watching for God to show up. If the guest does not come forward, then they simply approach them where they are standing.

In either case, at some point they ask the guest this question: "If God was to do a miracle in your life, what would it be?" This is an emotionally charged question that incites dramatic responses. The Shepherd's Staff team member asks to lead the guest in a prayer about that miracle. Invariably God shows up in that prayer and they are touched by His presence. This creates a spiritual bond. Then the team member asks to follow up with a phone call that week, just to see how the guest is doing and if there is any change in his or her miracle situation. During the phone call the guest is invited to coffee or lunch. If that doesn't happen, the guest is asked about receiving a Bible study (most of our guests check the "Bible Study" box on the guest card). If the guest declines, then at least an invitation back to church the next Sunday is extended. Obviously the intent of this follow-up is to establish a disciple-making relationship.

Home Bible Studies

Like many churches, we have emphasized and trained people to teach home Bible studies. We all understand that we cannot make any progress with anyone's move toward salvation without providing good biblical information so he or she can make an informed decision. We cannot lead anyone to the new birth without providing information in a way that he or she can understand it. Once the Bible study is finished, whether that person has been born again or not, there is always the "what now?" question. Some churches offer discipleship classes, which is the next logical step. But these classes alone do not make disciples. Some who received the Bible study may have not yet begun attending church services. In this case the student may consider continuing the relationship and Bible study.

If they have obeyed the gospel, then they should not be abandoned by the Bible study teacher. The transition from a Bible study into a discipleship relationship should be seamless. It takes a long time to make a saint of God, and spending several months if not up to one entire year in weekly Bible studies and life sharing is not too much time. If they have not obeyed the gospel, and if they are obviously hungry and eager to learn more, then the teacher should stay with them, transitioning into a disciple-making relationship. As of this writing I have been making a disciple with my literal neighbor for the last nine months. He has not been to our church one time and I have not invited him. I know someday he will come to church because I keep sowing the Word into his life. He keeps me encouraged to spend time with him because he asks the right questions, has a thankful heart, and is demonstrating transformation in his personal life.

These are just a few of the practical ways we have implemented disciple making in our church.

Conclusion

Thank you for your investment of time in reading this book. It is my sincere hope that at the least, I have provoked you to think carefully about the mission of the church, and at the most, I have influenced how you will proceed with the kingdom business of making disciples. I have been in full-time ministry for thirty-eight years, but I can tell you that since my eyes have been opened to the command of Jesus to go make disciples, my life has been changed. I now come to the text with a disciple maker's lens. Many verses have taken on a whole new context (as I have attempted to share in this work). My day feels a little empty, if not wasted, if I have not done at least one thing (great or small) to make a disciple. Sunday worship services are no longer a "pick me up" or an "emergency room" for the saints who come dragging in, but it is now a time to celebrate what we have been doing all week long through Christ to advance His kingdom.

Just so you know I am not a lab coat technician, I would like to conclude my thoughts by sharing with you some of my current disciple-making ventures. I decided that I would be more intentional about making a disciple out of my youngest son. He agreed to sit down with me every school morning the last two years and have a devotion together (he just graduated from high school last night). We only spent fifteen minutes together each time, but it was the last fifteen minutes every morning before he left for public school. We read a chapter in the Word together, and then we read a page or two from a biography of a Oneness Pentecostal hero of the faith from the twentieth century. We typically followed this with a short discussion about the day that lay before us and then a prayer. After several months of weighing his post–high school educational options, I am gratified and excited that he has decided to attend Urshan College and prepare for a lifetime of ministry. (God called him at the age of twelve.) I want my children to be my greatest and best disciples.

As of this writing I am engaged in three other weekly disciple-making relationships. I had coffee with one of my disciples last week (a backslider, only our second discipleship meeting). He told me his boss wanted to come and meet me and so we did this week. I was curious as to why his boss wanted to meet me, but he answered my question when he said, "There has been a dramatic change in (he said his name), and I had to come and meet the man who has made a difference." Obviously we give all the glory to God.

My second disciple relationship is with a family (husband, wife, young children) who have been coming to church fairly regularly for about two years. I taught him about baptism more than a year ago but he didn't seem interested. He had been baptized in another denominational church when he was young. I'm suspecting that perhaps he had a fear that a re-baptism would mean he was denying the faith of his parents. So imagine my surprise when someone sent me a video on my phone of his baptism last Sunday (I was out of town). When I asked him what pulled the trigger he said, "I don't know. It was just time." I suppose the message here is to never give up, keep the relationship close, and let the Word and prayer do the work.

I've mentioned my other disciple earlier in this book. At the time this book first went to press, I have been working with him weekly for fourteen months. Even before he was baptized in the tenth month of our disciple-making relationship he began to make dramatic lifestyle changes. He shared with me recently that others have noticed a change in him and have made comments to him about it. My heart's desire and passion for him is that he will walk in truth. I will do everything within my ability to see that it happens.

Questions for Discussion:

- What is a way that making disciples could be the overarching purpose of every existing ministry in your local church?

- How could your church upgrade its current model of visitor follow-up to become more intentional about disciple making?

- What is your plan to make a disciple once a Bible study is completed with a sinner or new believer?

SELECT BIBLIOGRAPHY

Coleman, Robert. *The Master Plan of Evangelism*. Grand Rapids, MI: Spire, 2010.

Damazio, Frank. *The Making of a Leader*. Portland, OR: Bible Temple Publishing, 1988.

French, Talmadge. *Our God Is One*. Indianapolis: Voice & Vision Publications, 1999.

Gallaty, Robert. *Growing Up: How to Be a Disciple Who Makes Disciples*. Bloomington, IN: Crossbooks, 2013.

Idleman, Kyle. *Not a Fan: Becoming a Completely Committed Follower of Jesus*. Grand Rapids, MI: Zondervan, 2011.

McCallum, Dennis and Jessica Lowery. *Organic Discipleship: Mentoring Others into Spiritual Maturity and Leadership*. Columbus, OH: New Paradigm, 2012.

Neighbor, Ralph Jr. *Where Do We Go From Here? A Guidebook for Cell Group Churches*. Houston: Touch Publications, 1990.

Ogden, Greg. *Discipleship Essentials: A Guide to Building Your Life in Christ*. Downers Grove, IL: InterVarsity Press, 2012.

Platt, David. *Follow Me: A Call to Die, a Call to Live*. Carol Stream, IL: Tyndale, 2013.

Platt, David. *Radical: Taking Back Your Faith from the American Dream.* Colorado Springs: Multnomah, 2010.

Synan, Vinson, ed. *Spirit-Empowered Christianity in the 21st Century.* Lake Mary, FL: Charisma House, 2011.